THE OFFICIAL DRIVER'S HANDBOOK

This booklet is a guide only. For official purposes, please refer to the Highway Traffic Act, the Motorized Snow Vehicles Act and the Off-Road Vehicles Act of Ontario.

Disponible en français
Demandez le «Guide officiel de l'automobiliste»

Driving is a privilege—not a right

PART ONE:
THE OFFICIAL
DRIVER'S
HANDBOOK

Introduction

Ontario's goal is to make its roads the safest in North America, and that's why the Ministry of Transportation has introduced a range of measures to improve the behaviour of all drivers, including new ones.

In 1999, more than 860 people were killed and more than 84,000 injured on Ontario roads. The social and economic costs of these collisions have been previously estimated at $9 billion annually.

Many collisions are caused by driver error — behaviour like following too closely, speed too fast, failure to yield the right of way, and improper turns and lane changes. And statistics show that new drivers of all ages are far more likely than experienced drivers to be involved in serious or fatal collisions.

Ontario campaigns against drinking and driving, aggressive driving and promoting the correct use of seat belts and child safety seats are making a difference. Graduated licensing, which lets new drivers gain skills and experience in low-risk environments, is also helping to develop better, safer drivers.

This section of the handbook gives new drivers the basic information they need about learning to drive in Ontario: the rules of the road, safe driving practices and how to get their licence to drive a car, van or small truck. The ministry recommends that all drivers would benefit from taking a course in advanced driver training.

As you read, remember that this is only a guide. For more detailed information about driving you can read the book Road Worthy, a driving textbook produced by the Ministry of Transportation. For official descriptions of the laws, look in the Highway Traffic Act of Ontario and its Regulations.

Information on how to get licences to drive other types of vehicles is available in Part Two of this handbook, the Motorcycle Handbook, the Official Truck Handbook, the Official Bus Handbook and the Official Air Brake Handbook.

CONTENTS — Part one

7

GETTING YOUR DRIVER'S LICENCE

This chapter tells you what licence you need to drive in Ontario and how to get it, whether you are a new driver, a visitor or a new resident in Ontario.

If you are applying for your first licence, this chapter explains the graduated licensing system, how to apply for a licence, the tests you will have to pass and the driving privileges you will have at each licence level.

What you need to drive in Ontario

If you live in Ontario, you must be at least 16 years old and have a valid Ontario driver's licence to drive in this province.

If you are a visitor to Ontario and want to drive while you are here, you must be at least 16 years old and have a valid driver's licence from your own province, state or country. If you are from another country and visiting Ontario for more than three months, you need an International Driver's Permit from your own country. If you don't have an International Driver's Permit, you can apply for an Ontario driver's licence.

If you are a new resident in Ontario and have a valid driver's licence from another province, state or country, you can use it for 60 days after you move to Ontario. If you want to keep driving in Ontario, you must get an Ontario driver's licence. Ontario has licence exchange agreements with every Canadian province and territory, the United States, Japan, Korea, Austria, Germany and Switzerland. Please see the section on new Ontario residents on page 17 for more information.

Quick check chart

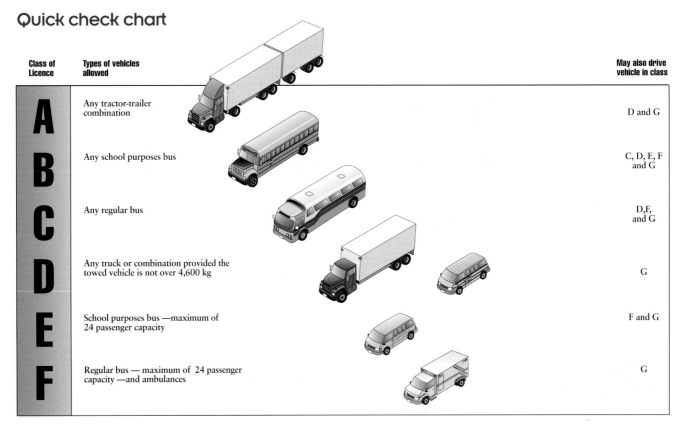

Class of Licence	Types of vehicles allowed	May also drive vehicle in class
A	Any tractor-trailer combination	D and G
B	Any school purposes bus	C, D, E, F and G
C	Any regular bus	D, F, and G
D	Any truck or combination provided the towed vehicle is not over 4,600 kg	G
E	School purposes bus —maximum of 24 passenger capacity	F and G
F	Regular bus — maximum of 24 passenger capacity —and ambulances	G

Class of Licence	Types of vehicles allowed
G	Any car, van or small truck or combination of vehicle and towed vehicle up to 11,000 kg provided the towed vehicle is not over 4,600 kg.
G1	Level One of graduated licensing Holders may drive Class G vehicles when accompanied by a fully licensed driver with at least four years of driving experience. Additional conditions apply.
G2	Level Two of graduated licensing Holders may drive Class G vehicles without accompanying driver but are subject to certain conditions.
M	Motorcycles Holders may also drive a Class G vehicle under the conditions that apply to a Class G1 licence holder.
M1	Level One of graduated licensing. Holders may drive a motorcycle under certain conditions.
M2	Level Two of graduated licensing Holders may drive a motorcycle but only with a zero blood alcohol level. Holders may also drive a Class G vehicle under the conditions that apply to a Class G1 licence holder.

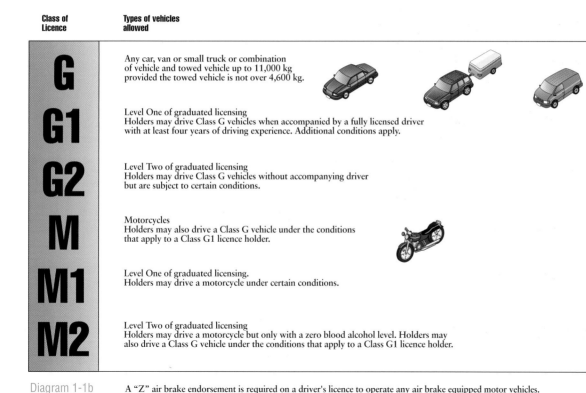

Diagram 1-1b   A "Z" air brake endorsement is required on a driver's licence to operate any air brake equipped motor vehicles.

What kind of licence?

In Ontario, there are 12 different kinds of licences. Each one qualifies you to drive a different type of vehicle. The class of licence you have must match the type of vehicle you are driving. You need a Class G licence to drive a car, van or small truck. You must have a Class G licence before you can be licensed to drive any other type of vehicle. The only exception is motorcycles. You may get a motorcycle licence (Class M) without first getting a Class G licence. The Quick Check Chart on page 10 shows you what class of licence you need to drive different vehicles.

For information on the skills and knowledge you'll need to get a Class M motorcycle licence, study the Official Motorcycle Handbook.

You can get information on other kinds of licences — classes A,B,C,D,E and F — in the Official Truck Handbook and the Official Bus Handbook. If you want to drive a vehicle equipped with air brakes, the Official Air Brake Handbook tells you how to qualify.

Some recreational vehicles have special licence requirements. If you plan to drive an off-road vehicle, snowmobile or moped, or pull a trailer, read the Off-Road Vehicles section in this Handbook.

You do not need a licence to ride a bicycle in Ontario.

Graduated licensing

As of April 1, 1994, new drivers applying for their first car or motorcycle licence enter Ontario's graduated licensing system. Graduated licensing lets new drivers get driving experience and skills gradually. The two-step licensing process takes at least 20 months to complete.

To apply for a licence, you must be at least 16 years old and pass a vision test and a test of your knowledge of the rules of the road and traffic signs. After you pass these tests, you will enter Level One and get a Class G1 licence. You may obtain a 'N' sign at the Driver Examination Centre for a nominal fee. You may hang the sign in the rear window (without obstructing your vision) of the vehicle you use to practice driving. The 'N' sign lets other drivers know you are a new driver.

You must pass two road tests to become fully licensed. Passing the first road test lets you move to Level Two (Class G2) and the second one gives you full Class G driving privileges.

Probationary drivers

Before graduated licensing, newly licensed drivers were called probationary drivers and had to complete two 12-month probationary periods without having their licences suspended. The probationary driver system will continue until all new drivers licensed before April 1, 1994 complete their probationary periods.

Applying for a licence

To apply for a licence, you must show proof of your identity and the date of your birth. Documents must be original. The following documents are acceptable.

For date of birth and personal identification: (Must state day, month and year of birth)

- passport
- citizenship card
- Canada Immigration Form 1000 (record of landing)
- Permanent Resident Document (as of Fall 1994)
- photo driver's licence (expired or from another area)
- National Defence photo identification card
- Indian Treaty card
- certificate of Indian status

- deposition signed by the superintendent of a training school operated by Public Safety and Security
- sealed security identification which includes photo, signature and date of birth

For date of birth only: (Must state day, month and year of birth)

- birth certificate
- driver's licence (expired or from another area)
- baptismal certificate with official seal of church
- baptismal certificate, without seal, accompanied by other identification showing date of birth
- sworn affidavit with supporting documents

For personal identification only:

(Must bear applicant's signature)
- age of majority card
- motor vehicle permit
- marriage certificate

- change of name certificate
- court order for name change
- certified adoption papers
- immigration card
- employee identification card
- student card
- credit card
- hospital card
- driver's licence photo (expired or from another area)
- membership card (such as library card, club membership)
- direct identification by a parent who has acceptable proof of identity and date of birth

Bring the documents to a Driver Examination Centre or Travel Point (a temporary driver examination centre where there is no regional centre). Phone ahead to find out where the nearest Travel Point is and when it is open. You will find the number under Driver and Vehicle Licence Information in the

Government of Ontario section of the blue pages in your phone book.

You must pay a fee when you apply. This fee includes the cost of the knowledge test and your first road test. There are more charges for your second road test and for any retests you may need to take.

When you apply for your licence, you will be asked questions about your health. People with some physical or medical conditions are not allowed to drive for safety reasons. If your physical or medical condition means you cannot be licensed, you will be told when you apply.

After you have a licence, you should report any change in your medical condition that may change your ability to drive safely. By law, doctors and optometrists must report the name and address of anyone over 16 who has a condition that may make it unsafe for him or her to drive.

Graduated licensing requirements

Here are the rules you must follow at each level:

Level One (Class G1):

Level One lasts 12 months. The Ministry of Transportation encourages all new drivers to take an approved driver education course to help learn the proper driving skills and knowledge. You should begin your training as soon as possible after becoming a Level One driver so you can get as much driving experience as you can. If you pass an approved course, you can complete Level One in eight months. While at Level One:

- You must not drive if you have been drinking alcohol. Your blood alcohol level must be zero.
- You must not drive alone. A fully licensed driver with at least four years of driving experience must sit in the front passenger seat. This is the only person who can be in the front seat with you while you drive. Your accompanying driver must have a Class G or higher licence and a blood alcohol level of less than .05 per cent.
- Each person in the vehicle must have a working seat belt.
- You must not drive on roads with a posted speed limit over 80 km/h including the 400-series highways, the Queen Elizabeth Way (QEW), the Don Valley Parkway (DVP), the Gardener Expressway, the E. C. Row Expressway, and the Conestoga Parkway in Kitchener-Waterloo. However, if your accompanying driver is a driving instructor licensed in Ontario, you may drive on any road.
- You must not drive between midnight and 5 a.m.

You must pass a road test of your driving skills to move to Level Two. At this time, you will be given a Class G2 licence.

Level Two (Class G2):

Level Two lasts at least 12 months. At this level you have more privileges because of your driving experience. At Level Two:

- You must not drive if you have been drinking alcohol. Your blood alcohol level must be zero.
- Each person in the vehicle must have a working seat belt.

After 12 months at Level Two, you may take a road test to qualify for full licence privileges. You must pass this test to get a Class G licence.

Road tests

Road tests check your driving skills in the vehicle and in traffic. You will be tested on your ability to apply the rules of the road and safe driving practices.

The Level One road test deals with basic driving skills. The Level Two road test deals with more advanced knowledge and driving skills. Your performance in each of the tests will tell you whether you need more training or practice.

When you feel qualified to drive safely and confident enough to take your road test, contact a Driver Examination Centre or the Road Test Booking Call Centre at (416) 325-8580 or 1-888-570-6110 to make an appointment. If you are unable to keep the appointment, phone the Driver Examination Centre or the Road Test Booking Call Centre to cancel your test.

You must bring a vehicle for each of your road tests. Make sure it is a vehicle you are familiar with and is in good working order. Bring your current licence to the appointment. If you are a Level One driver, a fully licensed driver with at least four years of driving experience must come to the test centre with you.

During the road tests, no pets or passengers other than the driver examiner are allowed in the vehicle. The examiner may stop or refuse to start the driving test if:

- your vehicle is not in good working order;
- you have been drinking alcohol or show any signs of impairment from alcohol or drugs;
- your driving skills are not good enough to finish the test without risking the safety of yourself, the examiner or other road users, including cyclists and pedestrians.

You will not be asked to do anything illegal during the road test. The examiner will explain the test and you should simply follow her or his instructions. The examiner is not allowed to coach you during the test, so if you have any questions, ask them before you begin.

While the Level One road test checks your basic driving skills, the Level Two road test is much more demanding. You should learn the proper driving skills as soon as possible after becoming a Level One driver so you can get as much driving experience as you can before taking the Level Two test.

For the Level Two test, you must demonstrate a high level of driving skill and knowledge. You will also have to show that you can drive well on a freeway or high speed highway.

While you are taking the test, the examiner will be watching to see how well you control your vehicle and perform such driving tasks as starting, stopping, turning, parallel parking and three-point turning. The examiner will check your observation skills, including when and how often you use the mirrors, where you look, and how you respond to traffic, signs, pavement markings and possible hazards.

You will be tested on how well you manage the space around your vehicle, your ability to make safe lane changes and how closely you follow and stop behind other vehicles. How you communicate with other road users — using turn signals and brake lights and making eye contact with other drivers and pedestrians — will also be noted, as well as the correctness of your driving decisions, such as knowing when to yield the right-of-way. For more information on the Level Two road test, see Chapter 6.

At the end of each test, the examiner will give you a complete report of your skills and explain any mistakes you have made. If you fail the test, the report will show you where you need to improve. When you have had more practice, you can make an appointment to take the test again. You must wait at least 10 days between tests.

New Ontario residents

If you are a new resident of Ontario and have a valid driver's licence from another province or country, you can use that licence for 60 days in Ontario. If you want to continue to drive after 60 days, you must get an Ontario driver's licence.

Drivers from Canada, the United States, Japan, Korea, Austria, Germany and Switzerland

If you are a licensed driver with two or more years of driving experience in another Canadian province or territory, the United States, Japan, Korea, Austria, Germany or Switzerland, you may get full Class G licence privileges without taking a knowledge test or any road test. However, you must meet all medical requirements, including a vision test, and show acceptable proof of your previous licence status and driving experience. These conditions also apply to licensed motorcycle drivers from Canada, the United States and Switzerland. There is no exchange agreement for motorcycle drivers from Japan, Korea, Austria or Germany. However, credit for holding a motorcycle licence from one of these countries will be granted for previous motorcycle experience

when applying for a Class M motorcycle licence in Ontario.

If you have less than two years of driving experience, you may get credit for your experience and enter Level Two of the graduated licensing system. Once you have a total of two years of driving experience, you may take the Level Two road test to earn full driving privileges.

Drivers from other areas

If you are a licensed driver from a country other than Canada, the United States, Japan, Korea, Austria, Germany or Switzerland, you must meet the Ontario driver medical requirements, pass a vision test and a test of your knowledge of the rules of the road and traffic signs.

If you have acceptable proof of two or more years of driving experience, you may take the Level Two road test to earn full driving privileges. If you do not pass this road test, you will

get a Level One (car or motorcycle) licence and may immediately schedule a Level One road test.

If you have less than two years of driving experience, you will be placed in Level One. However, if you have acceptable proof that you have the driving experience required for Level One, you can immediately schedule a Level One road test to enter Level Two.

If you do not have the driving experience required for Level One, you will stay in Level One until you do. You can then take the Level One road test to enter Level Two.

A driver's licence from another area is considered acceptable proof if it shows you have the driving experience required. If it does not, you will need to show documents that do.

If you do not have acceptable proof of your driving experience, you will start at the beginning of Level One as a new driver.

COULD YOU PASS?

The rest of this handbook gives you information you need to pass your tests and to keep your driving privileges once you get your licence.

Here is a sample question that could appear on the knowledge test:

If you are convicted of drinking and driving, you will lose your driver's licence on the first offence for a minimum of: (choose one) **1.** One month.   **2.** Three months.   **3.** Six months.   **4.** One year.

The test may also ask you about:
- seat belts
- traffic signs and lights
- emergency vehicles
- how to use headlights
- speed limits
- getting on or off a freeway
- what drivers must do when they meet streetcars and school buses
- driver licence suspensions
- the demerit point system
- passing other vehicles
- collision reporting

The road tests will test how well you use your knowledge. You will be tested on:
- starting, stopping and turning
- traffic signs and lights
- passing vehicles, including bicycles, and driving in passing lanes
- travelling through controlled and uncontrolled intersections
- parallel parking and reversing
- foreseeing hazardous conditions and being ready for them
- other safe driving practices.

Make sure you know the information in this handbook before you take these tests.

SAFE AND RESPONSIBLE DRIVING

Being a safe and responsible driver takes a combination of knowledge, skill and attitude.

To begin, you must know the traffic laws and driving practices that help traffic move safely. Breaking these "rules of the road" is the major cause of collisions.

Traffic laws are made by federal, provincial and municipal governments, and police from each level can enforce them. If you break a traffic law, you may be fined, sent to jail or lose your driver's licence.

But you need to do more than just obey the rules. You must care about the safety of others on the road. Everyone is responsible for avoiding collisions. Even if someone else does something wrong, you may be found responsible for a collision if you could have done something to avoid it.

Because drivers have to co-operate to keep traffic moving safely, you must also be predictable, doing what other people using the road expect you to do. And you must be courteous. Courteous driving means giving other drivers space to change lanes, not cutting them off and signalling your turns and lane changes properly.

Finally, you must be able to see dangerous situations before they happen and to respond quickly and effectively to prevent them. This is called defensive or strategic driving. There are collision avoidance courses available where you can practice these techniques.

Defensive driving is based on three ideas: visibility, space and communication.

Visibility is about seeing and being seen. You should always be aware of traffic in front, behind and beside you. Keep your eyes constantly moving, scanning the road ahead and to the side and checking your mirrors every five seconds or so. Make sure other drivers can see you too.

I. Getting ready to drive

Managing the **space** around your vehicle lets you see and be seen and gives you time and space to avoid a collision. Leave a cushion of space ahead, behind and to both sides. Because the greatest risk of a collision is in front of you, stay well back.

Communicate with other road users to make sure they see you and know what you are doing. Catch the eye of pedestrians, cyclists, and drivers at intersections and signal whenever you want to slow down, stop, turn or change lanes. If you need to get another person's attention, use your horn.

Before you drive, make sure you are comfortable with your physical and mental state, your vehicle and the conditions in which you will be driving. If you have doubts about any of them, don't drive.

Be physically and mentally alert

You must be in good physical and mental condition to drive.

Don't drive when you are sick or injured or when you have been drinking alcohol or taking any drug or medication that may reduce your ability to drive.

Don't drive when you are tired. You might fall asleep at the wheel, risking the lives of others on the road. Even if you don't fall asleep, fatigue affects your driving ability. Your thinking slows down and you miss seeing things. In an emergency, you may make the wrong decision or you may not make the right one fast enough.

Diagram 2-1

And don't drive when you are upset or angry. Strong emotions can reduce your ability to think and react quickly.

Know your vehicle

Get to know your vehicle before you drive it. There are many types of vehicles available today with many different characteristics including fuel ignition system, anti-lock brakes, 4-wheel drive, and systems for traction control and stability control. Check the vehicle owner's control. Check the vehicle owner's manual. For driving in difficult situations and conditions see the section on dealing with particular situations on page 57. The book Road Worthy can also help you with this.

Make sure you know where all the controls and instruments are and what they do. Check that all warning lights and gauges work. Watch for a warning light that stays on after you drive away; it could mean a serious problem with your vehicle.

Get to know the controls well enough to turn on wipers and washers, headlights, highbeams, heater and defroster without having to look. This is an important part of driving — learning to use simple controls without taking your eyes off the road.

Get into position

Make sure you sit properly behind the wheel. You should sit high enough in the driver's seat to see over the steering wheel and hood. You should be able to see the ground four metres in front of the vehicle. Use a firm cushion if needed.

Be sure that you are sitting straight upright in the seat with your elbows slightly bent. Adjust the seat so your feet reach the pedals easily. To check your position, try placing your feet flat on the floor under the brake pedal. If you can do this without stretching, you are seated properly. This keeps you in the proper, upright sitting position and gives you more stability when manoeuvring your vehicle.

If your vehicle has an adjustable headrest, you should make sure it is at the right height. The back of your head should be directly in front of the middle of the headrest to protect you in a collision.

Check that you have enough room in the front seat to drive properly and safely. Do not overcrowd your driving space with passengers or property.

Keep a clear view

Keep a clear view when driving. Do not put anything in your windows that will block your view. If you are a new driver using the 'N' sign in your rear window, be sure it does not block your view.

The windows of your vehicle should not be coated with any material that keeps you from seeing out in any direction. Neither should the windshield or front door windows be coated to keep someone from seeing inside the vehicle.

I. Getting ready to drive

Diagram 2-2

Find your blind spots

Check and adjust your mirrors and find your blind spots. When you use mirrors there is an area on each side of your vehicle where you cannot see. You may not see people, cyclists, or vehicles when they are in these spots.

Mirrors should be positioned so that there are as few blind spots for you as possible. Blind spots in most

vehicles are to the back left and back right of the vehicle. On some vehicles the blind spot is so large that a vehicle could be there and you would not see it. To reduce the blind spots, position the interior mirror so that the centre of the mirror shows the centre of the rear window. You should be able to see directly behind the car when the interior mirror is properly adjusted. Position the left outside mirror, by leaning towards the window and moving the mirror so that you can just see the rear of your car. Position the right outside mirror by leaning to the centre of the vehicle and moving the mirror so that you can again just see the rear of your car. Avoid overlap in what you can see in your mirrors. Because your side mirrors show only narrow angles of view, turning your head is the only way to make sure there is nothing in your blind spots.

You should know the blind spots on your own vehicle. You can learn where and how large they are by having someone walk around your car and watching the person in the mirrors.

Fasten your seat belt

Use your seat belt every time you travel in any vehicle equipped with seat belts. All passengers should be buckled up in their own seat belt or child seat.

Drivers who do not buckle up can be fined up to $500 and given two demerit points. (See page 104 for information about demerit points.) Drivers may also receive demerit points if they fail to ensure that passengers under 16 years of age are properly buckled in a seat belt or child car seat. Level One (G1) and Level Two (G2) drivers who do not wear a seat belt or who do not ensure there is a working seat belt for every passenger can lose their

Diagram 2-3

licence for 30 days. Never put more than one person into a seat belt; this can cause serious injury or even death in a collision.

Seat belts should be worn snug enough to keep you in your seat during a collision. Wear the shoulder strap over your shoulder, never under your arm. The lap belt should be worn low over the hips, not against the stomach.

Use your seat belt always, even when you are sitting in a position with an active airbag. Airbags do not replace seat belts. In a collision, your seat belt will keep you in position so that the airbag can protect you.

Note: The safest place a passenger can travel is inside a vehicle, properly buckled in. It is not safe to travel outside a vehicle, such as in the back of a pick-up truck, or in a trailer that is being towed. It is important for passengers to be secured within a vehicle to avoid being thrown from the vehicle during a collision.

For more information on seat belts call MTO INFO (416) 235-4686 (1-800-268-4686) or visit www.mto.gov.on.ca

Child Safety

To be safely protected in a vehicle, children must be properly secured in a child car seat, booster seat or seat belt, depending on their size and development.

As a driver, you are responsible for ensuring that passengers under 16 years of age are properly buckled into a seat belt or child car seat. The fine for not using a child car seat as required by law is up to $500 plus two demerit points.

Child car seats must meet Canadian Motor Vehicle Safety Standards (CMVSS). Buckles and straps must be fastened according to the manufacturer's instructions. Newer vehicles that come equipped with a lower anchorage or "ISOfix" system for securing a child car seat, do not require a seat belt to secure the child car seat to the vehicle.

I. Getting ready to drive

Diagram 2-4

Children 12 years of age and under are safest in the back seat, away from active air bags.

Infants that weigh less than nine kg or 20 lb. must be buckled into a rear-facing child safety seat attached to the vehicle by a seat belt. Do not put a rear-facing child car seat in a seat with an active airbag. If the airbag inflates, it could seriously injure the child.

Toddlers nine to 18 kg (20 to 40 lb.) travelling in their parent's vehicle must be buckled into a child safety seat attached to the vehicle both by a tether strap at the top and at the base by a seat belt. Always follow the manufacturer's instructions.

Children weighing more than 18 kg (40 lb.) who have outgrown forward-facing child seats but who are too small to benefit from the protection that a seat belt provides are safest using a booster seat. Use a high-back booster with a lap/shoulder belt or a regular vehicle booster with a lap belt alone.

Children weighing more than 18 kg (40 lb.) who are not in booster seats must use a seat belt. Make sure the shoulder belt fits snugly against the body with the lap belt fitting below the abdomen.

Correct installation of a child car seat is key for ensuring a child's safety. Your local public health unit is a good resource for finding out how to properly install a child car seat.

For more information on child car seats call MTO INFO (416) 235-4686 (1-800-268-4686) or visit www.mto.gov.on.ca

Note: Be careful if buying a used child car seat. Ensure that the seat does not show signs of deterioration, has not been in a collision, is not under recall, is not more than 10 years old, and that it comes with complete manufacturer's instructions and all necessary equipment.

SEAT BELTS AND CHILD CAR SEATS SAVE LIVES

Seat belts and child safety seats reduce the risk of injury or death in collisions.

- Seat belts help keep you inside and in control of the vehicle during a collision. People who are thrown from a vehicle have a much lower chance of surviving a collision.
- Seat belts keep your head and body from hitting the inside of the vehicle or another person in the vehicle. When a vehicle hits a solid object, the people inside keep moving until something stops them. If you are not wearing your seat belt, the steering wheel, windshield, dashboard or another person might be what stops you. This "human collision" often causes serious injury.
- Fire or sinking in water are rare in collisions. If they do happen, seat belts help keep you conscious, giving you a chance to get out of the vehicle.
- In a sudden stop or swerve, no one can hold onto a child who is not in a seat belt or child seat. Infants or children who are not wearing seat belts can be thrown against the vehicle's interior, collide with other people or be ejected.
- When using a child car seat, make sure that the seat is tightly secured by the vehicle seat belt or by the anchor bar with the ISOfix system. When installing the child car seat, kneel on top of the seat and use your body weight to push it into the vehicle seat and tighten the seat belt as much as possible. The installed child car seat should move no more than 2.5 cm (1 inch) away from the vehicle seat back.
- Use a locking clip where needed to ensure that the seat belt stays locked into position and will not develop slack during a collision.
- If a rear-facing car seat does not rest at the proper 45-degree angle, then you can prop up the base of the seat with a towel or a Styrofoam bar ("pool noodle"). Eighty per cent of the base of a forward-facing car seat should be firmly supported by the vehicle seat.

Turn on headlights at night and in poor conditions

Headlights make it easier for you to see and be seen at night and in poor light conditions. Your vehicle's headlights must shine a white light that can be seen at least 150 metres in front and is strong enough to light up objects 110 metres away. You must also have red rear lights that can be seen 150 metres away and a white light lighting the rear licence plate when headlights are on.

Turn on headlights one-half hour before sunset and keep them on until one-half hour after sunrise. You must always use lights when fog, snow or rain keeps you from clearly seeing people or vehicles less than 150 metres away. Please see the section on driving at night and in bad weather on page 61.

Don't drive with only one headlight or with lights that are not aimed properly. Have your headlight adjustment checked regularly, keep them clean, and replace burned-out bulbs as soon as possible.

Parking lights are only for parking. In low light, use your headlights, not parking lights.

When you use highbeam headlights, remember to switch to lowbeams within 150 metres of an oncoming vehicle. Use your lowbeams when you are less than 60 metres behind another vehicle unless you are passing it. These rules apply to all roads, including divided ones.

Studies show that using daytime running lights makes it easier for other drivers to see you. Remember to switch to regular headlights one-half hour before sunset.

Diagram 2-5: **Highbeams**

Diagram 2-6: **Lowbeams**

II. Driving along

Always be aware of traffic around you as you drive. Develop a routine for looking ahead, behind and from side to side. Check your mirrors every five seconds or so, and check your blind spots by turning your head to look over your shoulder. Keep other drivers out of your blind spot by changing your speed and don't drive in other vehicles' blind spots. Be extra careful at dusk and dawn when everyone has difficulty adjusting to the changing light.

Keep a cushion of space around your vehicle and be prepared for the unexpected. Anticipate other driver's movements and make allowances for every possible error. Look well ahead and watch for people in parked vehicles — they may be about to pull out in front of you or to open a door. Watch for smaller vehicles, bicycles and pedestrians.

Steer smoothly

All steering should be smooth and precise. You should do most steering and lane changes without taking either hand off the wheel. You should also be able to steer in a straight line while shifting gears, adjusting controls or checking your blind spot.

Picture the steering wheel as a clock and place your hands at nine o'clock and three o'clock or at 10 o'clock and two o'clock.

Use signals

Signals tell other drivers what you want to do, giving them a chance to co-operate.

Use your turn signals and brake lights to signal before stopping, slowing down, turning, changing lanes, leaving the road, or moving out from a parked position. Give the correct signal well before the action and make sure other drivers can see it. Check that the way is clear before

Left Turn

Right Turn

Slowing Down OR Stopping

Diagram 2-7

II. Driving along

you act — just signalling is not enough.

If your turn signals and brake lights are not working, use hand and arm signals. The pictures on page 27 show how to make hand and arm signals. When watching for signals made by others, remember that cyclists may signal right turns by holding their right arms straight out.

After signalling, move only when it is safe to do so.

Keep right

Keep to the right of the road or in the right-hand lane on multi-lane roads unless you want to turn left or pass another vehicle. This is especially important if you are driving more slowly than other vehicles.

Obey speed limits

Obey the maximum speed limit posted on signs along the road, but always drive at a speed that will let you stop safely. This means driving below the maximum speed in bad weather, in heavy traffic or in a construction zone.

Where there are no posted speed limits, the maximum speed is 50 km/h in cities, towns, villages and built-up areas and 80 km/h elsewhere.

Obey police

When police officers are directing traffic, you must follow their directions even if they are different from traffic lights or signs.

Bring your vehicle to a safe stop when a police officer signals you to pull over.

Keep a safe distance from other vehicles

As a general rule, drive at the same speed as traffic around you without going over the speed limit. Leave a cushion of space around your vehicle to let other drivers see you and to avoid a collision.

Whenever you follow another vehicle, you need enough space to stop safely if the other vehicle brakes suddenly. A safe following distance is at least two seconds behind the vehicle in front of you. This lets you see around the vehicle ahead and gives you enough distance to stop suddenly.

Do not block the normal and reasonable movement of traffic.

To give yourself a two-second space, follow these steps:

1. Pick a marker on the road ahead, such as a road sign or telephone pole.

2. When the rear of the vehicle ahead passes the marker, count "one thousand and one, one thousand and two".

3. When the front of your vehicle reaches the marker, stop counting. If you reach the marker before you count "one thousand and two," you are following too closely.

2 Seconds or More

Leave more than a two-second distance in bad weather and when following large vehicles that block your view of the road ahead. You will also need to leave more space when your vehicle is heavily loaded and when following smaller, lighter vehicles, such as motorcycles, that can stop more quickly than you.

Diagram 2-8

Diagram 2-9

Diagram 2-10

Sharing the road with other vehicles

Motorcycles, mopeds, motor assisted bicycles and bicycles are harder to see because of their size. Drivers of these vehicles may make sudden moves because of uneven road surfaces or poor weather conditions. And because they are less protected, they are more likely to be injured in a collision.

Drivers of motorcycles, mopeds, motor assisted bicycles and bicycles must obey the same rules of the road as car drivers. However, mopeds, motor assisted bicycles and bicycles that cannot keep up with traffic should drive as close as possible to the right edge of the road. For safety, cyclists should ride at least one metre away from parked vehicles and at least one-half metre away from the curb to avoid debris, potholes and sewer grates. If the lane is wide enough, you may share it with the cyclist, keeping a safe distance to the cyclist's left. If the lane is not wide enough to share, the cyclist has the right to use the whole lane.

Motorcycles use a full lane; treat them like other vehicles when driving. Since many motorcycle turn signals do not automatically shut off, be careful when turning left in front of an oncoming motorcycle with its turn signal on. Make sure the motorcyclist is turning and not going through your path having forgotten to switch off the turn signal.

Sharing the road with large vehicles

The length and width of large trucks can create special driving situations. For example, drivers of long trucks that are turning right may move into the left lane to avoid hitting the curb as they turn. If you ignore a truck's turn signals and pull up on its right side, you may be squeezed between the truck and the curb when the turn begins.

Most trucks need a longer distance to stop than cars. Signal well before turning, slowing or stopping to give trucks behind you enough time to brake. When stopped going uphill, a truck may roll back farther than a car when the driver releases the brake and engages the clutch. Leave at least one car length between your vehicle and the truck.

On some high-speed roads with more than two lanes in each direction, trucks longer than 6.5 metres cannot use the far left lane. Overhead signs mark these lanes. Trucks must use the lane to the right to pass slower vehicles, so try to keep this lane clear.

On some roads, buses have special stopping areas for dropping off and picking up passengers. You must let buses re-enter traffic from these areas.

Sharing the road with pedestrians

Pay special attention to pedestrians, whether they are crossing roads in traffic, walking or jogging alongside roads, or using crosswalks or pedestrian crossings. Elderly pedestrians or those with disabilities need extra caution and courtesy from drivers as they may be slow in crossing the road. Be alert for pedestrians who are blind, visually impaired, hearing impaired, people in wheel chairs or people walking slowly due to some other physical impairment and give them appropriate consideration. Pedestrians who are blind or visually impaired may use **a white cane or guide dog** to help them travel safely along

sidewalks and across intersections. Caution signs are posted in some areas where there is a special need for drivers to be alert.

Some streetcar stops have a special safety island or zone for passengers getting on and off. Pass these safety islands and zones at a reasonable speed. Always be ready in case pedestrians make sudden or unexpected moves.

III. Driving through intersections

Slow down as you come to intersections and look carefully for traffic, yield signs, stop signs, traffic lights, cyclists and pedestrians.

There are two main types of intersections: controlled and uncontrolled.

Controlled intersections

Controlled intersections have traffic lights, yield signs or stop signs to control traffic.

At a controlled intersection where you face a green light, drive carefully through the intersection at a steady speed. If the light has been green for a while, be prepared to stop when it turns yellow. However, if you are already so close that you cannot stop safely, drive through the intersection with caution. Where you face a red light, come to a complete stop and wait until the light turns green.

When you approach an intersection on a main road, and the road beyond the side street is blocked with traffic, stop before entering the intersection and wait until the traffic ahead moves on. This does not apply if you are turning left or right.

At a controlled intersection where you face a yield sign, slow down or stop if necessary and wait until the way is clear before driving through the intersection.

At a controlled intersection where you face a stop sign, come to a complete stop. Drive through the intersection only when the way is clear.

Uncontrolled intersections

Uncontrolled intersections have no signs or traffic lights. They are usually found in areas where there is not much traffic. Be extra careful around these intersections.

Diagram 2-11

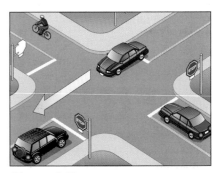

Diagram 2-12

If two vehicles come to an uncontrolled intersection from different roads at the same time, the driver on the left must let the driver on the right go first. This is called yielding the right-of-way.

Yielding the right-of-way

There are times when you must yield the right-of-way. This means you must let another person go first. Here are some rules about when you must yield the right-of-way.

At an intersection without signs or lights, you must yield the right-of-way to any vehicle approaching from the right (Diagram 2-11).

At an intersection with stop signs at all corners, you must yield the right-of-way to the first vehicle to come to a complete stop. If two vehicles stop at the same time, the vehicle on the left must yield to the vehicle on the right (Diagram 2-12).

Diagram 2-13

Diagram 2-14

At any intersection where you want to turn left or right, you must yield the right-of-way. If you are turning left, you must wait for approaching traffic to pass or turn and for pedestrians in your path to cross. If you are turning right, you must wait for pedestrians to cross if they are in your path (Diagram 2-13).

A yield sign means you must slow down or stop if necessary and yield the right-of-way to traffic in the intersection or on the intersecting road.

When entering a road from a private road or driveway, you must yield to vehicles on the road and pedestrians on the sidewalk (Diagram 2-14).

IV. Stopping

Diagram 2-15

You must yield the right-of-way to pedestrians crossing at specially marked pedestrian crossings or crossovers (Diagram 2-15).

Remember, signalling does not give you the right-of-way. You must make sure the way is clear.

Diagram 2-16

Diagram 2-17

Knowing how to stop safely and properly is an important driving skill. Good drivers see stops ahead, check their mirrors and begin brak-ing early, stopping smoothly. Braking is easier when you sit properly. Use your right foot for both brake and gas pedals so you won't step on both pedals at the same time or flash your brake lights unnecessarily. Press the brake pedal firmly and evenly.

In a vehicle with manual transmission, try shifting into a lower gear going down long, steep hills. This will help control your speed and you won't have to brake as sharply. Downshift before starting downhill since it may not be possible afterwards. As a guide, you should be in the same gear going downhill as uphill.

You must come to a complete stop at all stop signs and red traffic lights. Stop at the stop line if it is marked on the pavement (Diagram 2-16). If there is no stop line, stop at the crosswalk, marked or not. If there is no crosswalk, stop at the edge of the sidewalk. If there is no sidewalk, stop at the edge of the intersection **(Diagram 2-17).** Wait until the way is clear before entering the intersection.

Stopping at railway crossings

All railway crossings on public roads in Ontario are marked with large red and white 'X' signs. Watch for these signs and be prepared to stop. You may also see signs warning of railway crossings ahead. On private roads, railway crossings may not be marked, so watch carefully.

As you come to a crossing, slow down, listen and look both ways to make sure the way is clear before crossing the tracks. If a train is coming, stop at least five metres from the nearest rail. Do not cross the track until you are sure all trains have passed.

Some railway crossings have flashing signal lights and some use gates or barriers to keep drivers from crossing the tracks when a train is coming.

At a railway crossing where the signal lights are flashing, stop at least five metres from the nearest rail. Do not cross until the signals stop flashing. If the crossing has a gate or barrier, wait until it rises or opens before crossing. It is dangerous and illegal to drive around, under or through a railway gate or barrier while it is being opened or closed.

Buses and other public vehicles are required to stop at railway crossings that are not protected by gates or signal lights. School buses must stop at railway crossings whether or not they are protected by gates or signal lights. Watch for these buses and be prepared to stop behind them.

Be careful in heavy traffic not to drive onto a railway crossing if you may have to stop on the tracks. Always make sure there is enough space to drive across the tracks completely before you begin to cross.

Diagram 2-18

IV. Stopping

Stopping at school crossings

You must stop for school crossing guards guiding children across a road. These guards carry red and white stop signs. Drivers who don't stop can be fined.

Stopping for school buses

All school buses in Ontario, whatever their size, are chrome yellow and display the words 'School Bus'.

No matter what direction you are travelling in, you must stop whenever you approach a stopped school bus with its upper alternating red lights flashing, unless you are on a road with a median. In that case only vehicles coming from behind must stop. (A median is a raised, lowered or earth strip dividing a road where vehicles travel in both directions.) Coming from the opposite direction, stop at a safe distance for children to get off the bus and cross the road in front of you. If you are coming from behind the bus, stop at least 20 metres away. Do not go until the bus moves or the lights have stopped flashing.

You must obey the school bus law on any road, no matter how many lanes or what the speed limit. Be prepared to stop for a school bus at any

Diagram 2-19

Diagram 2-20

time, not just within school hours.

As well as the upper alternating red flashing lights, school buses use a stop sign arm on the driver's side of the bus. This arm, a standard stop sign with alternating flashing red lights at top and bottom, swings out after the upper alternating red lights begin to flash. Do not go until the arm folds away and all lights stop flashing.

If you don't stop for a school bus, you can be fined $400 to $2,000 and get six demerit points for a first offence. If you break the rule a second time within five years, the penalty is a fine of $1,000 to $4,000 and six demerit points. You could also go to jail for up to six months.

Watch for school buses near railway crossings. All school buses must stop at all railway crossings. The upper alternating red lights are not used for these stops, so be alert.

Diagram 2-21

Stopping for pedestrian crossings
Pedestrian crossings — also called "crossovers" — let pedestrians safely cross roads where there are no traffic lights. Always watch for pedestrians and people using wheelchairs near these crossings. At some crossings, pedestrians can push a

V. Changing directions

button to make overhead yellow lights flash; at all crossings, pedestrians should point across the road to show they want to cross. Drivers, including cyclists, must stop and let all pedestrians cross. Once people have cleared your side of the road you can go with caution.

Do not pass any vehicle within 30 metres of a pedestrian crossing.

Before you turn a corner, back up or turn around, always check your mirrors and over your shoulder to make sure the way is clear and you have enough space to complete the move safely.

Turning a corner

To turn a corner, signal well before the turn. When the way is clear, move into the proper lane — either the far right lane for a right turn or the far left lane in your direction for a left turn. Signal your turn and look from side to side to make sure the way is clear.

Slow down before you enter the turn; the sharper the turn, the slower you should go. To keep full control of the turn, finish braking before you turn the steering wheel.

For a sharp turn, turn the steering wheel with one hand and cross the other hand over it. Grip the wheel on the other side and continue turning. This is called "hand over hand steering." When you have completed the turn, relax your grip on the steering wheel and let it slip or gently feed it through your hands to return to the straight-ahead position. Do not turn the steering wheel with one finger or the flat palm of your hand.

Gradually increase speed as you complete the turn.

Remember, drivers lose control of vehicles and skid because they try to do more than one thing at a time. Try not to brake and steer at the same time.

Diagram 2-22

Right turns

Unless signs or pavement markings tell you not to, always begin and end a right turn close to the right side of the road.

To make a right turn, signal well before the turn and move into the right-hand lane when the way is clear. If the right-hand lane is not marked, keep as far to the right of the road as possible. Look ahead, left, right and left again before starting to turn. If you may not have seen any smaller vehicles

or pedestrians, check your right rear blind spot. Let cyclists or moped riders go through the intersection before you turn. When it is safe, make your turn into the right-hand lane of the road.

Right turn on a red light

Unless a sign tells you not to, you may turn right on a red light as long as you first come to a complete stop and wait until the way is clear. Remember to yield to pedestrians and others using the road.

Left turns

Unless signs or pavement markings tell you not to, always begin and end a left turn in the far left lane in your direction.

To make a left turn, signal well before the turn and move into the far left lane when the way is clear. Look ahead, left, right and left again and check your blind spot. Make your turn when the way is clear.

When you are stopped at an intersection waiting for approaching traffic to clear, don't turn your steering wheel to the left until you can complete the turn. With your wheels turned to the left, your vehicle could be pushed into the path of oncoming traffic.

When two vehicles coming from opposite directions meet in an intersection waiting to turn left, each should turn to the left of the other after yielding the right-of-way to pedestrians and oncoming traffic.

Motorcycles, bicycles and mopeds turn left at intersections in the same way as larger vehicles. If you are making a left turn behind one of these vehicles, do not pull up beside it to make your turn at the same time. Stay behind and turn when the way is clear. Wait for the smaller vehicle to move right before you pass.

The following diagrams show you the correct way to turn left on different types of roads:

V. Changing directions

Diagram 2-23: **Two-way road to a two-way road.**

Turn from the lane closest to the centre line to the lane right of the centre line, following a smooth arc. Then, when you can, move into the right curb lane.

Diagram 2-25: **One-way road to a two-way road.**

Turn from the left curb lane to the lane just right of the centre line. Then, when you can, move into the right curb lane.

Diagram 2-24: **Two-way road to a one-way road.**

Turn from the lane closest to the centre line to the left curb lane.

Diagram 2-26: **One-way road to a one-way road.**

Turn from the left curb lane to the left curb lane.

Left-turn lanes

Some roads have special lanes for vehicles turning left (Diagram 2-27). At an intersection where left-turn lanes are marked on the pavement, make your turn from the marked lane. Keep this lane position as you turn onto the other road.

The centre lane of some roads is used as a two-way left-turn lane (Diagram 2-28). This lets left-turning vehicles from both directions wait for a chance to turn without holding up traffic. To use a two-way left-turn lane, follow these steps:

1. Signal and move into the centre lane shortly before your turn. Slow down.
2. Carefully move forward to a spot opposite the road or driveway where you want to turn.
3. Make your turn when the way is clear.

Diagram 2-27

Remember that vehicles from the opposite direction also use this lane to turn left. As they wait in front of you, it may be hard for you to see oncoming traffic. Only go when you are sure the way is clear.

Left turn on a red light

You may turn left from a one-way road to a one-way road on a red light after coming to a complete stop and making sure the way is clear. Yield to pedestrians and traffic.

Diagram 2-28

V. Changing directions

Backing up

Take extra care and move slowly when backing up (reversing) your vehicle. Before you begin, check that the way is clear behind you. Be especially careful to look for children and cyclists. Put the gear selector in reverse and turn sideways in your seat to look over your shoulder in the direction you are moving, while holding the steering wheel firmly.

If you are reversing straight back or to the right, turn your body and head to the right and look back over your right shoulder (**Diagram 2-29**). When reversing to the left, turn your body and head to the left and look over your left shoulder (**Diagram 2-30**). Always check the opposite shoulder as well. If you are turning as you reverse, check that the front end of your vehicle does not hit anything.

You don't have to wear a seat belt while backing up. If you need to remove your seat belt to turn your

Diagram 2-29

Diagram 2-30

body to see properly when reversing, do so. But don't forget to buckle up again before moving forward.

It is illegal to drive in reverse on a divided road that has a speed limit of more than 80 km/h. This applies to the travelled section of the road and the shoulder. The only exception to this rule is if you are trying to help someone in trouble.

Turning around

You may need to turn around when driving if you miss a turn or go too far along a road. There are several ways to do this safely.

The simplest and safest way is to drive around the block, but there may be times when this is not possible. In such cases, a U-turn or a three-point turn may be necessary.

U-turn

Before you make a U-turn, check to make sure there is no sign saying not to.

To make a U-turn safely, you must be able to see well in both directions. It is illegal to make a U-turn on a curve in the road, on or near a railway crossing or hilltop, or near a bridge or tunnel that blocks your view. Never make a U-turn unless you can see at least 150 metres in both directions.

To make a U-turn, signal for a right turn, check your mirror and over your shoulder and pull over to the right side of the road. Stop. Signal a left turn and when traffic is clear in both directions, move forward and turn quickly and sharply into the opposite lane. Check for traffic as you turn.

Three-point turn

On narrow roads you need to make a three-point turn to change directions. As shown in Diagram 2-31, a three-point turn starts from the far right side of the road.

Signal for a left turn. When the way is clear in both directions, move forward, turning the steering wheel sharply left towards the curb on the far side of the road. When you have reached the left side of the road, stop, and put the vehicle into reverse. Signal a right turn. After checking that the way is still clear, turn the steering wheel sharply to the right, while backing up slowly to the other side of the road. Stop. Shift to forward gear and check traffic. When the way is clear, drive forward.

Diagram 2-31

VI. Changing positions

Changing your position on the road involves changing lanes or overtaking and passing another vehicle. Before beginning, be sure you have enough space and time to complete the move safely.

Changing lanes

Changing lanes is a sideways movement from one lane to another on roads with two or more lanes in the same direction. You may want to change lanes to overtake another vehicle, to avoid a parked vehicle or when the vehicle ahead slows to turn at an intersection.

Never change lanes without giving the proper signal and looking to make sure the move can be made safely.

Here are the steps for making a lane change.
1. Check your mirrors for a space in traffic where you can enter safely.
2. Check your blind spot by looking over your shoulder in the direction of the lane change. Signal that you want to move left or right.
3. Check again to make sure the way is clear and that no one is coming too fast from behind or from two lanes over on a multi-lane road.
4. Steer gradually into the new lane. Do not slow down — maintain the same speed or gently increase it.

Never make sudden lane changes by cutting in front of another vehicle, including bicycles. Other drivers expect you to stay in the lane you are already in. Even if you signal, they expect you to yield the right-of-way.

MAKE SURE SIGNAL IS OFF

MAKE GRADUAL CHANGE

CHECK AGAIN

CHECK BLIND SPOT AND SIGNAL

CHECK FOR SAFE SPACE GAP

Diagram 2-32

Avoid unnecessary lane changes or weaving from lane to lane. You are more likely to cause a collision, especially in heavy traffic or bad weather. Don't change lanes in or near an intersection. Remember that spending a few seconds behind another vehicle is often safer than going around it.

Passing

Passing is changing lanes to move past a slower vehicle. Although all roads have speed limits, not all vehicles travel at the same speed. For example, cyclists, vehicles working on the road and drivers preparing to turn are usually slower than the main traffic. You will likely want to pass some slow-moving vehicles when you are behind them.

Never overtake and pass another vehicle unless you are sure you can do so without danger to yourself or others. Don't pass moving snow plows under any conditions. If in doubt, do not pass.

Here are the steps for passing a vehicle:

1. Use your left-turn signal to show that you want to pass and check that the way is clear ahead and behind before moving into the passing lane.
2. Watch out for bicycles and small vehicles that may be hidden from view in front of the vehicle you are about to pass. Also watch for vehicles that may be turning left in front of you and vehicles or pedestrians entering the road from another road or driveway.
3. Change lanes only after signalling. After overtaking, signal that you want to move back into the lane you started from, and when you can see all of the front of the vehicle you are passing in your rear view mirror, make the lane

Diagram 2-33

VI. Changing positions

change. Be careful not to cut off a vehicle by suddenly moving in front of it.

4. If the vehicle you are passing speeds up, do not race. Go back to your original lane. And do not speed up when another driver is trying to pass you. It is rude and dangerous.

Do not pass within 30 metres of a pedestrian crossing.

When passing parked vehicles, watch carefully for people suddenly opening doors or for doors opened to load and unload.

Motorcycles, bicycles and mopeds often need to pull to the left or right side of their lane to avoid dangerous road conditions or to be seen by other drivers. Do not take this as an invitation to pass in the same lane. If you do want to pass these vehicles, do so by changing lanes.

When another vehicle wants to pass you, you must move to the right and let it pass. When being passed on an undivided road where the passing driver has pulled into the opposite lane, pay attention to oncoming traffic and move closer to the right side of the lane. Be prepared to slow down to let the passing driver get in front of you more quickly to prevent a collision.

On many high-speed roads with three or more lanes in each direction, trucks are not allowed to drive in the far left-hand lane. This means that the lane next to it is the truck passing lane. If you are in this lane and a truck wants to pass, move into the right-hand lane as soon as you can.

Diagram 2-34

Passing at night

Be very careful when you pass other vehicles at night. If you have to pass and the way is clear, follow these steps:

1. Switch your headlights to low beams as you approach a vehicle from behind.
2. Switch your highbeams on and off quickly to warn the driver ahead you are going to pass.
3. Signal, check your mirrors and blind spot, and pull out to pass. As you move alongside the vehicle you are passing, switch on your highbeams. This will let you see more of the road ahead.
4. When you can see all of the front of the vehicle you are passing in your rear view mirror, you are far enough ahead to pull back into the right lane. Remember to signal.

Diagram 2-35

Passing and climbing lanes

Some high-speed roads have special passing or climbing lanes. These lanes let slower vehicles move into the right-hand lane so that faster ones can pass safely in the left lane.

An advance sign tells drivers they will soon have a chance to pass. Another sign warns when the lane is ending so drivers in the right-hand lane can begin to merge safely with traffic in the left-hand lane.

VI. Changing positions

Passing on the shoulder

You may drive on the right shoulder only to pass a vehicle turning left and only if the shoulder is paved. The exception to this is when you are directed by a person controlling traffic on the road to pass on the right or when the operator of a vehicle working on the road signals you to pass on the right and you can do so safely. You may not pass on the left shoulder, paved or not.

Passing on the right

Most passing is done on the left. You may pass on the right on multi-lane or one-way roads and when overtaking a streetcar or a left-turning vehicle.

Passing on the right can be more dangerous than passing on the left. If you are driving in the passing lane with a slower vehicle in front of you, wait for the vehicle to move to the right. Do not suddenly change lanes and pass on the right; the driver in front may realize

you want to pass and move to the right at the same time you do.

Passing streetcars

You must pass streetcars on the right unless you are driving on a one-way road.

At streetcar stops, stay at least two metres behind the rear doors where passengers are getting off or on.

This rule does not apply at stops where an area has been set aside for streetcar passengers. Always pass these areas at a reasonable speed and be prepared for pedestrians to make sudden or unexpected moves.

Diagram 2-36

VII. Parking

Since parking rules change from road to road and place to place, always watch for and obey signs that say you may not stop or limit stopping, standing or parking. Be aware that not all parking by-laws are posted on signs.

Here are some basic parking rules:

- Never park on the travelled part of a road. Drive off the road onto the shoulder if you must stop for some reason.
- Never park on a curve, hill or anywhere you do not have a clear view for at least 125 metres in both directions.
- Do not park where you will block a vehicle already parked or where you will block a sidewalk, crosswalk, pedestrian crossing or road entrance.
- Do not park within three metres of a fire hydrant, on or within 100 metres of a bridge or within six metres of a public entrance to a hotel, theatre or public hall when it is open to the public.

- Do not park within nine metres of an intersection or within 15 metres if it is controlled by traffic lights.
- Do not park within 15 metres of the nearest rail of a level railway crossing.
- Do not park where you will get in the way of traffic or snow clearing.

- Never open the door of your parked vehicle without first making sure that you will not endanger any other person or vehicle or interfere with traffic. When you must open a door next to traffic, keep it open only long enough to load or unload passengers.

Diagram 2-37

PARKING FOR PEOPLE WITH DISABILITIES

The Disabled Person Parking Permit, issued by the Ministry of Transportation, replaced disabled symbol licence plates and municipal parking permits in 1990.

The portable permit may be used in any vehicle in which a driver or passenger with a disability is travelling. A vehicle displaying the permit and carrying a person with a disability (either as driver or passenger) may park in designated spaces. Ontario, all other Canadian provinces, and most American states recognize the permit.

The permit is available, free of charge, to eligible applicants. To be eligible, you must be unable to walk more than 200 metres without serious difficulty or danger to safety or health. You must show a medical certificate from a licensed physician, chiropractor, osteopathic physician, physiotherapist or occupational therapist. Temporary permits are also available for people with a disability lasting more than two months but not permanent. Companies and organizations that provide transportation regularly to people with disabilities can also apply for permits. Application forms are available at any Driver and Vehicle Licence Offices.

It is illegal to park in a parking space for people with disabilities unless you have an official parking permit and are transporting the permit holder. You must display the permit on the sun visor or dashboard in the windshield of the vehicle.

If your permit is due to expire on or after March 01, 2002, you will get a renewal notice and an application form in the mail approximately three months in advance. Complete the top portion of the application form and have your doctor complete the bottom portion. Then take the completed form to a Driver and Vehicle Licence Office, or mail it to the Ministry of Transportation, P. O. Box 9200, Kingston, Ont. K7L 5K4. The ministry will send you a new permit. When you get it, destroy your old permit and display the new one.

You could be fined $50 to $2,000 under municipal by-laws for unlawfully parking in a designated space. These parking spaces are marked with a Disabled Person Parking Permit sign.

VII. Parking

- Never park in a space designated for people with disabilities unless you display a Disabled Person Parking Permit in the windshield of your vehicle. The permit must belong to you or one of your passengers. This also applies to standing or stopping at curb areas reserved for picking up and dropping off passengers with disabilities.

After parking your vehicle, always turn off the ignition and the lights, remove the key and lock the door to stop theft. Do not leave children or animals in the vehicle.

Before moving from a parked position, always signal and check for traffic, pulling out only when it is safe to do so.

Parallel parking

Parallel parking means parking vehicles in a line, front to rear, next to the curb or side of the road. Park parallel to the curb on roads where parking is allowed unless there are signs saying that vehicles should be parked at an angle. Park on the right side of the road in the direction of traffic. Unless there are signs saying otherwise, you can parallel park on both sides of a one-way road.

To parallel park on the right-hand side of the road, find a space that is about one and half times longer than your vehicle. Check the traffic beside and behind and signal your wish to pull over and stop. Drive alongside — or parallel to — the vehicle ahead of the empty space, leaving about a metre between the vehicles. Stop when your rear bumper is in line with the other vehicle. 1) Slowly and carefully

Parking Permit

Province of Ontario / Province de l'Ontario

Permit No. / N° du permis

Expires at end of / Expire à la fin de

This side of the permit must be clearly visible from outside of vehicle:
- place on the dashboard, or
- attach to the turned-down sunvisor

Ce côté du permis doit être visible de l'extérieur du véhicule. Il peut être :
- déposé sur le tableau de bord; ou
- attaché à un pare-soleil abaissé

Minister of Transportation
Ministre des Transports

Permis de stationnement

Diagram 2-38

VII. Parking

Diagram 2-39

reverse into the space, turning the steering wheel fully towards the curb. **2)** When you can see the outside rear corner of the vehicle in front of your space, straighten your wheels as you continue to reverse. **3)** Then turn the steering wheel fully toward the road to bring your vehicle in line with the curb. **4)** If your vehicle is not parallel to the curb, drive forward to straighten. **5)** When you are properly parked, set the parking brake and move the gear selector into park, or shift into first or reverse gear if your vehicle has a manual transmission. Turn off the engine. Remember to remove the key from the ignition. Check traffic before opening your door. Lock your vehicle.

Parking on a hill

When parking facing downhill, turn your front wheels towards the curb or right shoulder. This will keep the vehicle from rolling into traffic if the brakes become disengaged (Diagram 2-40 A).

Turn the steering wheel to the left so the wheels are turned towards the road if you are facing uphill with a curb. The tires will catch the curb if it rolls backward (Diagram 2-40 B).

Facing uphill without a curb, turn the wheels sharply to the right. If the vehicle rolls, it will go off the road rather than into traffic (Diagram 2-40 C).

When parking on a hill, always set the parking brake and move the gear selector into park, or shift into first or reverse gear if your vehicle has a manual transmission. Turn off the engine and remove the key. Check for traffic before opening the door and remember to lock your vehicle.

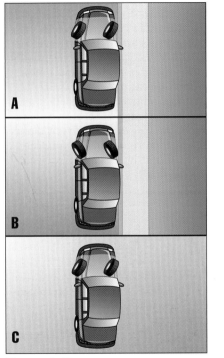

Diagram 2-40

Roadside stop

When you need to stop by the side of the road for a short time — to check something outside your vehicle or to look for directions on a map, for example — follow these directions.

Signal that you want to pull over and check your mirrors and blind spot to see when the way is clear. Steer to the side of the road, stopping close to the curb or edge of the road.

If your vehicle has an automatic transmission, put the gear selector in park and set the parking brake. If your vehicle has a manual transmission, set the parking brake and shift into neutral if not turning off the engine, or shift into low or reverse if turning off the engine. Turn on your four-way emergency flashers. When parking on a hill, turn your wheels in the appropriate direction to keep your vehicle from rolling.

When pulling out from a roadside stop, turn off your flashers, release the parking brake and move the gear selector to drive or shift into first gear. Signal and check your mirrors and blind spot to make sure the way is clear of vehicles and cyclists before driving back onto the road.

VIII. Freeway driving

A freeway — also called an express-way — is a high-speed, multi-lane road. On a freeway, traffic going in each direction is separated and special ramps let vehicles enter and exit. Vehicles travel faster on a freeway than on other roads, so driving can be more demanding and difficult. However, because there are no intersections, bicycles or pedestrians, freeway driving can be safer for experienced drivers.

New drivers need to learn how to drive with other vehicles around them at low speeds before trying freeway driving. Class G1 drivers may only drive on freeways with a licensed driving instructor.

Entering a freeway

There are usually two parts to a freeway entrance: an entrance ramp and an acceleration lane. In this lane, drivers raise their speed to the common speed of traffic on the freeway before they merge with it.

As you move along the freeway entrance ramp, look ahead and check your mirrors and blind spots to assess the traffic to see where you will move into the nearest freeway lane.

As you leave the ramp and enter the acceleration lane, signal and increase your speed to merge smoothly with traffic. Freeway drivers should move over, if it is safe to do so, leaving room for merging vehicles.

A few entrance ramps join the freeway on the left. This means you enter the fastest lane of traffic first. Use the acceleration lane to match your speed to the traffic, increasing your speed more quickly.

Diagram 2-41

Driving along a freeway

Once on the freeway, a good safety-conscious driver moves at a steady speed, looking forward and anticipating what's going to happen on the road ahead. Traffic should keep to the right, using the left lanes for passing.

As in city driving, your eyes should be constantly moving, scanning the road ahead, to each side and behind. Look ahead to where you are going to be in the next 15 to 20 seconds, or as far ahead as you can see, when you travel at faster speeds. Remember to keep scanning and check your mirrors frequently.

Stay clear of large vehicles. Because of their size, they block your view more than other vehicles. Leave space around your vehicle. This will let you see clearly in every direction and will give you time and space to react. (See page 29 for correct following distances.)

Be careful not to cut off any vehicle, large or small, when making a lane change or joining the flow of traffic. It is dangerous and illegal for a slower moving vehicle to cut in front of a faster moving vehicle.

Use the far left lane of a multi-lane freeway to pass traffic moving slower than the speed limit, but don't stay there. Drive in the right-hand lane when possible. On many freeways with three or more lanes in each direction, trucks cannot travel in the far left lane and must use the lane to the right for passing. Get into the habit of driving in the right lane, leaving the other lanes clear for passing.

Leaving a freeway

There are usually three parts to a freeway exit: a lane for slowing down that leads drivers out of the main flow of traffic, an exit ramp

Diagram 2-42

and an intersection with a stop sign, a yield sign or traffic light.

When leaving the freeway, signal that you want to move into the slowing lane, but do not slow down. When you are in the lane, reduce your speed gradually to the speed shown for the exit ramp. Check your speedometer to make sure you are going slowly enough. You may not realize how fast you are going because you are used to the high speed of the freeway. Be prepared to stop at the end of the exit ramp.

Signs tell you that there are freeway exits ahead far enough in advance for you to make any lane changes safely. If you miss an exit, do not stop or reverse on the freeway. Take the next exit.

HIGHWAY HYPNOSIS

Driving for a long time can be boring, especially at night or when you drive at the same speed for long distances. You can become "hypnotized" where everything seems to float by and you pay less attention to what is happening around you. You may even fall asleep.

You can help prevent highway hypnosis by following a few simple rules:
1. Don't eat a heavy meal before you drive.
2. Wear comfortable clothing.
3. Talk with your passengers, but not to the point of distraction.
4. Keep your eyes moving and check your mirrors often.
5. Take an interest in all road signs and traffic around you.
6. Take a coffee or walking break every hour.
7. Don't try to drive too far in one day.
8. Avoid driving during your normal sleeping hours.
9. Keep the temperature in your vehicle cool.

If you do start to become drowsy, do something different immediately. Open a window; talk to passengers; sing out loud; move your body around a bit.

Stop at the next service centre or rest area and take a short walk or have a coffee and eat a light snack. If you don't feel any more alert, find a place to sleep for an hour or for the night.

IX. Dealing with particular situations

Workers on the road

Be extra careful when driving through construction zones and areas where people are working on or near the road.

When approaching a construction zone, slow down and obey all warning signs and people who are directing traffic through the area. In the construction zone, drive carefully and adjust your speed and driving to suit the conditions. Obey posted speed limits, do not change lanes, be ready for sudden stops and watch for workers and construction vehicles on the road and give them more room to ensure everyone's safety.

Traffic control people are used at work zones to control vehicle traffic and prevent conflicts between construction activity and traffic. Whether you are driving during the day or at night, watch for traffic control people and follow their instructions.

Treat people working on roads with respect and be patient if traffic is delayed. Sometimes traffic in one direction must wait while vehicles from the other lane pass through a detour. If your lane is blocked and no one is directing traffic, yield to the driver coming from the opposite direction. When the way is clear, move slowly and carefully around the obstacle.

Animals on the road

You may come upon farm animals or wild animals on the road, especially in farming areas and in the northern parts of the province.

Animal crossing signs warn drivers where there is a known danger of large animals, such as moose, deer or cattle, stepping onto the road, but small animals may appear anywhere. Always be alert for animals and ready to react.

Look well ahead. At night, use your highbeams where possible. When you see an animal, brake or slow down if you can without risk to vehicles behind you. If there is no traffic and no danger of colliding with any other object, steer around the animal, staying in control of your vehicle.

In some areas of the province horse-drawn carriages may use the road. Be prepared to share the road with them.

IX. Dealing with particular situations

Cellular phones

Cellular phones can be an important safety aid for drivers. Many people use their phones to report crimes and collisions and for personal safety when they are lost or their vehicle breaks down.

But using a cellular phone while driving takes a driver's attention from the business of driving. Distracted drivers are more likely to make a driving error or to react too slowly. As more and more people use cellular phones, it is important that they be used safely.

Make it a habit to use your cellular phone only when you are parked, or have a passenger use the phone. If you are driving and your phone rings, let your cellular voice mail service take the call and listen to the message later when you are parked.

If you must use a cellular phone when driving, use a hands-free microphone. Make sure your phone is easy to see and reach and that you know how to use it. Use voice-activated or speed dialing and never take notes while driving.

Currently, there is no law against using a cellular phone while driving, but you can be charged with dangerous or careless driving if you cause a collision while using one.

Driver distractions

Driving is a job that requires your full attention every time you get behind the wheel. As a driver, you must always remember to reduce distractions and focus on your driving. Your first responsibility is to road safety.

There are a number of possible driver distractions including:

- **Using technology devices such as cell phones, laptops or hand-held organizers**
- **Reading maps, directions or other material**
- **Grooming (combing hair, putting on make-up or shaving)**
- **Eating or drinking**
- **Taking notes**
- **Talking with passengers**
- **Tending to children or pets**
- **Adjusting the controls in your vehicle (radio, CD player or climate control)**

Careless driving is a serious offence. Police can charge drivers with careless driving if drivers do not pay full attention to their driving. If you are convicted of careless driving, you will get six demerit points and can be fined up to $1,000 and sentenced to up to six months in jail. In some cases, your licence may be suspended for up to two years. **This is one of Ontario's toughest rules of the road.**

TIPS TO REDUCE DRIVER DISTRACTIONS

- Attend to personal grooming and plan your route before you leave.

- Identify and preset your vehicle's climate control, radio and CD player.

- Make it a habit to pull over and park to use your cell phone or have a passenger take the call or let it go to voice mail.

- Put reading material in the trunk if you are tempted to read.

- Do not engage in emotional or complex conversations. Stress can also affect your driving performance.

- When you are hungry or thirsty, take a break from driving.

Remember to focus on your driving at all times. A split-second distraction behind the wheel can result in injury or even death.

IX. Dealing with particular situations

Emergency vehicles

Watch for stopped emergency vehicles on shoulders of highways and when approaching reduce your speed. On highways with two or more lanes, move over to the adjacent lane, if possible.

If you hear the bell or siren of a police, fire, ambulance or public utility emergency vehicle, or see its lights flashing, you must get out of the way. On a two-way road, stop as close as possible to the right-hand side of the road and clear of any intersection. On a one-way road with more than two lanes, stop as close as possible to the nearest edge of the road and clear of any intersection. Wait until the emergency vehicle has passed.

It is illegal to follow an on-duty fire vehicle or ambulance within 150 metres in any lane going in the same direction.

Some volunteer firefighters use a flashing green light if they have to use their personal vehicles to respond to a fire. Courteous drivers yield the right-of-way to these vehicles.

Diagram 2-43

X. Driving at night and in bad weather

At night and in weather conditions such as rain, snow or fog, you cannot see as far ahead, even with headlights. Slow down when driving at night, especially on unlit roads, and whenever weather conditions reduce your visibility.

Overdriving your headlights

You are overdriving your headlights when you go so fast that your stopping distance is farther than you can see with your headlights. This is a dangerous thing to do, because you may not give yourself enough room to make a safe stop. Reflective road signs can mislead you as well, making you believe you can see farther than you really can. This may cause you to overdrive your headlights if you are not careful.

Glare

Glare is dazzling light that makes it hard for you to see and be aware what others around you are doing. It can be a problem on sunny and overcast days, depending on the angle of the sun's rays and your surroundings. Glare can also be a problem at night when you face bright headlights or see them reflected in your rear view mirror.

When meeting oncoming vehicles with bright headlights at night, look up and beyond and slightly to the right of the oncoming lights. In daytime glare, use your sun visor or keep a pair of good quality sunglasses in your vehicle. When you enter a tunnel on a bright day, slow down to let your eyes adjust to the reduced light. Remove your sunglasses and turn on your headlights.

Cut down glare at night by following the rules of the road for vehicle lights. Use your lowbeam headlights within 150 metres of an oncoming vehicle or when following a vehicle within 60 metres. On country roads, switch to lowbeams when you come to a curve or hilltop so you can see oncoming headlights and won't blind oncoming drivers. If you can't see any headlights, switch back to highbeams.

Diagram 2-44

TIPS FOR SAFE DRIVING IN FOG

Before you drive — and during your trip — check weather forecasts. If there is a fog warning, delay your trip until it clears, if possible. If you are caught driving in fog, follow these safe driving tips:

DO:
- Slow down gradually and drive at a speed that suits the conditions.
- Make sure the full lighting system of your vehicle is turned on.
- Use your lowbeam headlights. Highbeams reflect off the moisture droplets in the fog, making it harder to see.
- If you have fog lights on your vehicle, use them, in addition to your lowbeams. They could save your life.
- Be patient. Avoid passing, changing lanes and crossing traffic.
- Use pavement markings to help guide you. Use the right edge of the road as a guide, rather than the centre line.
- Increase your following distance. You will need extra distance to brake safely.
- Look and listen for any hazards that may be ahead.
- Reduce the distractions in your vehicle. For example, turn off the cell phone. Your full attention is required.
- Watch for any electronically-operated warning signs.
- Keep looking as far ahead as possible.
- Keep your windows and mirrors clean. Use your defroster and wipers to maximize your vision.
- If the fog is too dense to continue, pull completely off the road and try to position your vehicle in an area protected from other traffic. Turn on your emergency flashers.

DON'T:

- Don't stop on the travelled portion of the road. You could become the first link in a chain-reaction collision.
- Don't speed up suddenly, even if the fog seems to be clearing. You could find yourself suddenly back in fog.
- Don't speed up to pass a vehicle moving slowly or to get away from a vehicle that is following too closely.

REMEMBER:

- Watch your speed. You may be going faster than you think. If so, reduce speed gradually.
- Leave a safe braking distance between you and the vehicle ahead.
- Remain calm and patient. Don't pass other vehicles or speed up suddenly.
- Don't stop on the road. If visibility is decreasing rapidly, pull off the road into a safe parking area and wait for the fog to lift.
- When visibility is reduced, use your lowbeam lights.

Fog

Fog is a thin layer of cloud resting on the ground. Fog can reduce visibility for drivers, resulting in difficult driving conditions.

The best thing to do is to avoid driving in fog. Check weather forecasts and if there is a fog warning, delay your trip until it clears. If that is not possible or you get caught driving in fog, there are a number of safe driving tips you should follow. See tips for safe driving in fog on the opposite page.

If visibility is decreasing rapidly, move off the road and into a safe parking area to wait for the fog to lift.

X. Driving at night and in bad weather

Rain

Rain makes road surfaces slippery, especially as the first drops fall. With more rain, tires make less contact with the road. If there is too much water or if you are going too fast, your tires may ride on top of the water, like water skis. This is called hydroplaning. When this happens, control becomes very difficult. Make sure you have good tires with deep tread, and slow down when the road is wet.

Rain also reduces visibility. Drive slow enough to be able to stop within the distance you can see. Make sure your windshield wipers are in good condition. If your wiper blades do not clean the windshield without streaking, replace them.

In rain, try to drive on clear sections of road. Look ahead and plan your movements. Smooth steering, braking and accelerating will reduce the chance of skids. Leave more

space between you and the vehicle ahead in case you have to stop. This will also help you to avoid spray from the vehicle ahead that can make it even harder to see.

Stay out of puddles. A puddle can hide a large pothole that could damage your vehicle or its suspension, or flatten a tire. The spray of water could splash nearby pedestrians or drown your engine, causing it to stall. Water can also make your brakes less effective.

Flooded roads

Try not to drive on flooded roads — water may prevent your brakes from working. If you must drive through a flooded stretch of road, test your brakes afterwards to dry them out.

Test your brakes when it is safe by stopping quickly and firmly at 50 km/h. Make sure the vehicle stops in a straight line, without

pulling to one side. The brake pedal should feel firm and secure, not spongy — that's a sign of trouble. If you still feel a pulling to one side or a spongy brake pedal even after the brakes are dry, you should take the vehicle in for repair immediately.

Skids

A skid happens when your wheels slide out of control on a slippery surface. Skids can involve the front, rear or all four wheels. Most skids result from driving too fast for road or traffic conditions. Sudden, hard braking, going too fast around a corner or accelerating too quickly can cause your vehicle to skid or roll over.

Once in a skid, steer in the direction of the skid. To do this, look where you want your vehicle to go and steer toward that spot. Be careful not to oversteer. If you are on ice, skidding in a straight line, step on the clutch or shift to neutral.

Threshold braking — Threshold braking should bring you to a reasonably quick controlled stop in your own lane, even in slippery conditions. Brake as hard as you can without locking up or skidding the wheels. Press down on the brake pedal, trying to get as much braking power as possible. Then, if you feel any of the wheels locking up, release the brake pressure slightly and re-apply. Don't pump the brakes. Continue braking this way until you have brought the vehicle to a complete stop. Some vehicles have anti-lock brake systems that give you a maximum threshold stop automatically.

Anti-lock brakes — If your vehicle has an anti-lock braking system, practice emergency braking to understand how your vehicle will react. It is a good idea to practise doing this under controlled conditions with a qualified driving instructor.

Anti-lock braking systems, which are also called ABS, are designed to sense the speed of the wheels on a vehicle. An abnormal drop in wheel speed, which indicates potential wheel lock, causes the brake force to be reduced to that wheel. This is how the anti-lock braking system prevents tire skid and the accompanying loss of steering control. This improves vehicle safety during heavy brake use or when braking with poor traction.

Although anti-lock braking systems help to prevent wheel lock, you should not expect the stopping distance for your vehicle to be shortened. Under normal driving conditions, on clean dry roads, you will notice no difference between vehicles with anti-lock braking and vehicles without anti-lock braking.

Some drivers, unfamiliar with anti-lock braking, are surprised by the vibration that happens when they brake hard in an emergency. Make sure you know what to expect so you can react quickly and effectively in an emergency.

Snow

Snow may be hard-packed and slippery as ice. It can also be rutted, full of hard tracks and gullies. Or it can be smooth and soft. Look ahead and anticipate what you must do based on the conditions. Slow down on rutted, snowy roads. Avoid sudden steering, braking or accelerating that could cause a skid.

Whiteouts

Blowing snow may create whiteouts where snow completely blocks your view of the road. When blowing snow is forecast, drive only if necessary and with extreme caution.

TIPS FOR DRIVING IN BLOWING SNOW AND WHITEOUT CONDITIONS

Before you drive – and during your trip – check weather forecasts and road reports. If there is a weather warning, or reports of poor visibility and driving conditions, delay your trip until conditions improve, if possible. If you get caught driving in blowing snow or a whiteout, follow these safe driving tips:

DO:
- Slow down gradually and drive at a speed that suits the conditions.
- Make sure the full lighting system of your vehicle is turned on.
- Be patient. Avoid passing, changing lanes and crossing traffic.
- Increase your following distance. You will need extra space to brake safely.
- Stay alert. Keep looking as far ahead as possible.
- Reduce the distractions in your vehicle. Your full attention is required.
- Keep your windows and mirrors clean. Use defroster and wipers to maximize your vision.
- Try to get off the road when visibility is near zero. Pull into a safe parking area if possible.

DON'T:
- Don't stop on the travelled portion of the road. You could become the first link in a chain-reaction collision.
- Don't attempt to pass a vehicle moving slowly or speed up to get away from a vehicle that is following too closely.

REMEMBER:
- Watch your speed. You may be going faster than you think. If so, reduce speed gradually.
- Leave a safe braking distance between you and the vehicle ahead.
- Stay alert, remain calm and be patient.
- If visibility is decreasing rapidly, do not stop on the road. Look for an opportunity to pull off the road into a safe parking area and wait for conditions to improve.
- If you become stuck or stranded in severe weather, stay with your vehicle for warmth and safety until help arrives. Slightly open a window for ventilation. Run your motor sparingly. Use your emergency flashers.
- Be prepared and carry a winter driving survival kit that includes items such as warm clothing, non-perishable energy foods, flashlight, shovel and blanket.

Ice

As temperatures drop below freezing, wet roads become icy. Sections of road, in shaded areas or on bridges and overpasses, freeze first. It is important to look ahead, slow down and anticipate.

If the road ahead looks like black and shiny asphalt, be suspicious. It may be covered by a thin layer of ice known as black ice. Generally, asphalt in the winter should look gray-white in colour. If you think there may be black ice ahead, slow down and be careful.

XI. Dealing with emergencies

Snow plows

Snow removal vehicles are equipped with flashing blue lights that can be seen from 150 metres. A flashing blue light can only be used on snow removal vehicles.

Flashing blue lights warn you of wide and slow-moving vehicles: some snow plows have a wing that extends as far as three metres to the right of the vehicle. On freeways, several snow plows may be staggered across the road, clearing all lanes at the same time by passing a ridge of snow from plow to plow. Do not try to pass between them. This is extremely dangerous because there is not enough room to pass safely, and the ridge of wet snow can throw your vehicle out of control.

If you drive often or travel alone, you need to be ready to deal with emergencies. The Ontario Provincial Police video Travelling Alone gives many valuable safety tips. While the video is aimed at women, the information is useful for everyone. Contact your local OPP detachment for more information.

Here are some suggestions for coping with some common road emergencies:

If your brakes fail

Try pumping the brake pedal to temporarily restore hydraulic brake pressure. If this does not work, apply the parking brake gently but firmly while holding the release button. It is a good idea for new drivers to practise a parking brake emergency stop under controlled conditions with a qualified driving instructor. Total brake failure is very rare on modern vehicles. If your brakes do fail and

you manage to stop, do not drive away. Call for help.

If your gas pedal sticks

First try to lift the pedal by slipping your foot under it. Do not reach down with your hands while the vehicle is moving. If this does not work, turn on your four-way emergency flashers, shift to neutral and stop as soon as you safely can, preferably off the road. Turn off the ignition and do not drive away. Call for help.

If your headlights go out

Check the switch immediately. If the lights stay out, turn on your four-way emergency flashers and bring your vehicle to a safe stop, off the road. Call for help. It is dangerous and illegal to drive at night without lights.

If you have trouble on a freeway

At the first sign of trouble, begin to pull over. Do not wait for your vehicle to stall on the freeway. Check your mirrors, put on your four-way emergency flashers, slow down, and pull over to the nearest shoulder as quickly as possible. Never stop in the driving lanes.

Be careful getting out of your vehicle. If possible, leave through the door away from traffic. If you need help, get back in the vehicle and put a "Call Police" sign in the side or back window. If you do not have a "Call Police" sign, tie a white cloth around the antenna. Do not raise the hood.

While you wait for help, stay in your vehicle with the doors locked. If someone stops to help, ask them to call the police or automobile club for you. If you have a cellular phone, call for help yourself.

The Queen Elizabeth Way, the 400-series freeways, and many other high-speed roads are patrolled by the Ontario Provincial Police. Stay with your vehicle and help will arrive shortly.

If your wheels go off the pavement

Don't panic. Grip the steering wheel firmly. Take your foot off the gas pedal to slow down. Avoid heavy braking. When the vehicle is under control, steer toward the pavement. Be prepared to correct your steering and increase speed when your wheels are fully back on the pavement.

If a tire blows out

Blowouts can cause tremendous steering and wheel vibration, but don't be alarmed. Take your foot off the gas pedal to slow down and steer the vehicle firmly in the direction you want to go. Bring the vehicle to a stop off the road.

In a collision where someone is injured

St. John Ambulance recommends that all drivers carry a well-stocked first aid kit and know how to use it. Think about reading a book about first aid or sign up for a first aid course. It could mean the difference between life and death in a collision.

Every driver involved in a collision must stay at the scene or return to it immediately and give all possible assistance. If you are not personally involved in a collision, you should stop to offer help if police or other help has not arrived.

In a collision with injuries, possible fuel leaks or serious vehicle damage, stay calm and follow these steps:
- Call for help or have someone else call. By law, you must report any collision to the police when there are injuries or damage to vehicles or other property exceeding $1,000.

XI. Dealing with emergencies

- Turn off all engines and turn on emergency flashers. Set up warning signals or flares or have someone warn approaching drivers.
- Do not let anyone smoke, light a match or put flares near any vehicle in case of a fuel leak. If any of the vehicles is on fire, get the people out and make sure everyone is well out of the way. If there is no danger of fire or explosion, leave injured people where they are until trained medical help arrives.
- If you are trained in first aid, treat injuries in the order of urgency, within the level of your training. For example, clear the person's airway to restore breathing, give rescue breathing or stop bleeding by applying pressure with a clean cloth.
- If you are not trained in first aid, use common sense. For example, people in collisions often go into shock. Cover the person with a jacket or blanket to reduce the effects of shock.

- Stay with injured people until help arrives.
- Disabled vehicles on the road may be a danger to you and other drivers. Do what you can to make sure everyone involved in a collision is kept safe.

In a collision where no one is injured

Follow these steps in a collision where there are no injuries:

1. If the vehicles are driveable, move them as far off the road as possible — this should not affect the police officer's investigation. This is especially important on busy or high-speed roads where it may be dangerous to leave vehicles in the driving lanes. If you cannot move the vehicles off the road, set up warning signals or flares far enough away to give other traffic time to slow down or stop.

2. Call police (provincial or local, depending on where the collision takes place). By law, you must report any collision to the police when there are injuries or damage to vehicles or property exceeding $1,000.

3. Give all possible help to police or anyone whose vehicle has been damaged. This includes giving police your name and address, the name and address of the registered owner of the vehicle, the vehicle plate and permit number and the liability insurance card.

4. Get the names, addresses and phone numbers of all witnesses.

5. If damage is less than $1,000, you are still required by law to exchange information with anyone whose vehicle has been damaged. However, the collision does not have to be reported to the police.

6. Contact your insurance company as soon as possible if you intend to make a claim.

XII. Protecting the environment

Vehicles powered by gasoline and diesel give off air pollutants and gases such as oxides of carbon, nitrogen and sulphur, hydrocarbons and soot. These pollutants affect the quality of the air we breathe, our health, crop yields and even the global climate.

Hydrocarbons and oxides of nitrogen react in sunlight to form ground level ozone, better known as smog. Smog is a major health hazard responsible for respiratory ailments and other illnesses. Oxides of sulphur and nitrogen combine with water vapour to form acid rain, which damages our lakes, forests and crops.

Global warming is the result of too much carbon dioxide and other gases trapping heat in our atmosphere. Global warming could cause average temperatures to rise, causing droughts, crop failures, lower water levels and more frequent and severe storms.

A car gives off less carbon dioxide than a larger vehicle, such as an airplane, truck, bus or train, does. However, because so many people own cars and drive them so often, cars are responsible for nearly half the carbon dioxide produced by all forms of transportation. Vehicles that carry large numbers of passengers, such as buses, produce less carbon dioxide per passenger than cars.

As a driver, you can help to protect the environment from the harmful effects of driving by following these suggestions. Many of them can also save you money.

Before you drive:
- Plan ahead. Combine several errands into one trip.
- Avoid driving during rush hours. Driving in off-peak times takes less time, using less fuel and releasing fewer emissions.

- Pay attention to Smog Alerts. It is especially important to follow these suggestions on days when smog is bad.
- For short trips, consider walking or cycling.
- For longer trips, public transit is an environmentally friendly alternative to driving alone.
- Carpool whenever possible. If you want to meet at a central location, there are free carpool lots in many parts of the province. To find one near you, call MTO INFO (416) 235-4686 (1-800-268-4686).

While driving:
- Avoid starting your vehicle unnecessarily. A large burst of pollutants is emitted when a cold engine is started.
- Turn off your vehicle if parked more than 10 seconds. Even in cold weather, vehicle engines warm up within 30 seconds.

XII. Protecting the environment

- Obey the speed limits. Driving at high speed uses more fuel and increases your chances of a serious collision.
- On the freeway, use your vehicle's overdrive gear and cruise control for better fuel efficiency.
- Remove unnecessary weight from your vehicle, such as heavy baggage, wet snow and winter sand or salt.
- Maintain your vehicle's aerodynamics. Remove roof racks and compartments when not in use. At high speeds, use your vents instead of opening the windows.
- Use your vehicle's air conditioning wisely. Use your windows and vents in city and stop-and-go traffic. At high speeds, using your air conditioning is usually more fuel efficient than opening your windows and reducing the vehicle's aerodynamics.

- Don't 'top-off' the tank when refueling. Spilled fuel releases harmful vapours.

At the garage:
- Regular maintenance will keep your vehicle running at maximum efficiency, reducing the fuel you need to buy and the pollutants your vehicle emits.
- Keep your vehicle's engine well tuned. Worn spark plugs, dragging brakes, low transmission fluid or the transmission not going into high gear can increase fuel consumption substantially.
- Follow the recommended maintenance schedule in your vehicle owner's manual to maximize fuel efficiency.
- Have any fluid leaks checked by a specialist to avoid engine damage and harming the environment.

- Keep your tires properly inflated to reduce your fuel bill, emissions and tire wear.
- Have your vehicle's alignment checked regularly to reduce uneven tire wear and fuel consumption.

(See the section on maintaining your vehicle on page 112.)

10 WAYS YOU CAN HELP MAKE ONTARIO'S ROADS THE SAFEST IN NORTH AMERICA

1. Don't drink and drive. Don't drive when you're taking medication that will affect your driving.

2. Always wear your seat belt.

3. Obey the speed limits. Slow down when road and weather conditions are poor.

4. Don't take risks: don't cut people off in traffic, make sudden lane changes or run yellow lights.

5. Don't drive when you're tired, upset or sick.

6. If you're in doubt, let the other driver go first — yield the right-of-way.

7. Keep a two-second space between your vehicle and the one ahead. To check your distance: start counting when the vehicle ahead passes a fixed object, stop counting when your vehicle reaches the same spot.

8. Cut the distractions: don't overcrowd the vehicle or play loud music.

9. Always check your blind spot: look in your mirror and over your shoulder before you change lanes.

10. Check traffic in all directions before going into an intersection.

CHOOSING A DRIVING SCHOOL

As a new driver, choosing professional driving instruction may be the best way to put yourself safely in the driver's seat.

A driver training course or high school driver education program approved by the provincial government can teach you the skills and attitudes you need to be a safe and responsible driver. You may also be eligible to take your road test sooner and to save money on insurance premiums.

As well as teaching the basics, driver training emphasizes strategic driving techniques, risk perception and management, freeway driving, night driving and driving in adverse conditions. Most programs are designed for new drivers, but many schools also provide courses and services to upgrade your skills.

If you graduate from an approved program, the certificate you get will reduce the time you must spend at Level One by four months. It may also earn you savings on your car insurance.

Approved high school driver education programs offer in-class and in-car training after school for a fee. Courses are administered by the local school board, a principal or other high school authority. They are taught in high school classrooms by qualified instructors.

Approved driver training courses in Ontario must offer at least 25 hours of classroom training and 10 hours of behind-the-wheel training. Look for a program that offers high quality instruction and a comfortable learning environment. The school should also be equipped with up-to-date videotapes, overheads and other visual aids.

To help you choose the best driving school and course for you, use this checklist of features.

- Course information package
- Personalized program
- Classroom facilities
- Low student/teacher ratio
- Audio visual equipment
- In-vehicle topics covered
- Basic manoeuvres
- Strategic driving
- Risk perception and management
- Freeway driving
- Night driving
- Driving in adverse conditions
- Instructor qualifications and experience
- Regular instructor upgrading
- Student progress and evaluation reports
- Certificate of completion
- Minimum 25 classroom and 10 behind-the-wheel instruction hours
- Training materials
- Use of vehicle for road test
- Certification fee
- Registered educational institution
- Tuition receipts
- Testimonials
- Number of years in business
- Consumer protection insurance

TRAFFIC SIGNS AND LIGHTS

Traffic laws include the traffic signs and lights, pedestrian signals and pavement markings that tell drivers and other road users what they must do in certain situations. This chapter shows you what many of those signs, lights and markings look like and explains what they mean to drivers.

I. Signs

Traffic signs give you important information about the law, warn you about dangerous conditions and help you find your way. Signs use different symbols, colours and shapes for easy identification.

Here are some of the many signs you will see on Ontario roads:

A stop sign is eight-sided and has a red background with white letters. It means you must come to a complete stop. Stop at the stop line if it is marked on the pavement. If there is no stop line, stop at the crosswalk, marked or not. If there is no crosswalk, stop at the edge of the sidewalk. If there is no sidewalk, stop at the edge of the intersection. Wait until the way is clear before entering the intersection.

A school zone sign is five-sided and has a blue background with white symbols. It warns that you are coming to a school zone. Slow down, drive with extra caution, and watch for children.

I. Signs

A yield sign is a triangle with a white background and a red border. It means you must let traffic in the intersection or close to it go first. Stop if necessary and go only when the way is clear.

A railway crossing sign is X-shaped with a white background and red outline. It warns that railway tracks cross the road. Watch for this sign. Slow down and look both ways for trains. Be prepared to stop.

There are four other kinds of signs: regulatory, warning, temporary conditions, and information and direction.

Regulatory signs

These signs give a direction that must be obeyed. They are usually rectangular or square with a white or black background and black, white or coloured letters.

A sign with a green circle means you may or must do the activity shown inside the ring. A red circle with a line through it means the activity shown is not allowed.

Here are some common regulatory signs:

This road is an official bicycle route. Watch for cyclists and be prepared to share the road with them.

You may park in the area between the signs during the times posted. (Used in pairs or groups.)

Snowmobiles may use this road.

Do not enter this road.

 Do not stop in the area between the signs. This means you may not stop your vehicle in this area, even for a moment. (Used in pairs or groups.)

 Do not stand in the area between the signs. This means you may not stop your vehicle in this area except while loading or unloading passengers. (Used in pairs or groups.)

 Do not park in the area between the signs. This means you may not stop your vehicle except to load or unload passengers or merchandise. (Used in pairs or groups.)

 Do not turn left at the intersection.

 Do not drive through the intersection.

 Do not turn to go in the opposite direction. (U-turn)

 Do not turn right when facing a red light at the intersection.

 Do not turn left during the times shown.

 This parking space is only for vehicles displaying a valid Disabled Person Parking Permit.

 No bicycles allowed on this road.

I. Signs

 No pedestrians allowed on this road.

 Slow traffic on multi-lane roads must keep right.

 These signs, above the road or on the pavement before an intersection, tell drivers the direction they must travel. For example: the driver in lane one must turn left; the driver in lane two must turn left or go straight ahead; and the driver in lane three must turn right.

 Keep to the right of the traffic island.

 The speed limit in this zone is lower during school hours. Observe the speed limit shown when the yellow lights are flashing.

 Speed limit changes ahead.

 Traffic may travel in one direction only.

 This is a pedestrian crossing or crossover. You must yield the right-of-way to pedestrians.

 Do not pass on this road.

This sign, above the road or on the ground, means the lane is only for two-way left turns.

These signs mean lanes are only for specific types of vehicles, either all the time or during certain hours. Different symbols are used for the different types of vehicles. They include: buses, taxis, vehicles with three or more people and bicycles.

Keep to the right lane except when passing on two-lane sections where climbing lanes are provided.

This sign reserves curb area for vehicles displaying a valid Disabled Person Parking Permit picking up and dropping off passengers with disabilities.

I. Signs

Warning signs

These signs warn of dangerous or unusual conditions ahead such as a curve, turn, dip or sideroad. They are usually diamond-shaped and have a yellow background with black letters or symbols.

Here are some common warning signs:

Intersection ahead. The arrow shows which direction of traffic has the right-of-way.

Drivers on the sideroad at the intersection ahead don't have a clear view of traffic.

Posted under a curve warning, this sign shows the maximum safe speed for the curve.

Sharp bend or turn in the road ahead.

Narrow bridge ahead.

Pavement narrows ahead.

Chevron (arrow-head) signs are posted in groups to guide drivers around sharp curves in the road.

Road branching off ahead.

Slight bend or curve in the road ahead.

Winding road ahead.

The bridge ahead lifts or swings to let boats pass.

 Paved surface ends ahead.

 Bicycle crossing ahead.

 Stop sign ahead. Slow down.

 Share the road with oncoming traffic.

 Pavement is slippery when wet. Slow down and drive with caution.

 Hazard close to the edge of the road. The downward lines show the side on which you may safely pass.

 The road ahead is split into two separate roads by a median. Keep to the right-hand road. Each road carries one-way traffic.

 Right lane ends ahead. If you are in the right-hand lane you must merge safely with traffic in the lane to the left.

I. Signs

 Traffic lights ahead. Slow down.

 Snowmobiles cross this road.

 Bump or uneven pavement on the road ahead. Slow down and keep control of your vehicle.

 Steep hill ahead. You may need to use a lower gear.

 Traffic travels in both directions on the same road ahead. Keep to the right.

 Railway crossing ahead. Be alert for trains. This sign also shows the angle at which the railway tracks cross the road.

 Two roads going in the same direction are about to join into one. Drivers on both are equally responsible for seeing that traffic merges smoothly and safely.

 Underpass ahead. Take care if you are driving a tall vehicle. Sign shows how much room you have.

 Sharp turn or bend in the road in the direction of the arrow. The checkerboard border warns of danger. Slow down; be careful.

Deer regularly cross this road; be alert for animals.

 Watch for pedestrians and be prepared to share the road with them.

 This sign warns you that you are coming to a hidden school bus stop. Slow down, drive with extra caution, watch for children and for a school bus with flashing red lights.

 Truck entrance on the right side of the road ahead. If the sign shows the truck on the left, the entrance is on the left side of the road.

 Watch for fallen rock and be prepared to avoid a collision.

 Shows maximum safe speed on ramp.

 There may be water flowing over the road.

 These signs warn of a school crossing. Watch for children and follow the directions of the crossing guard or school safety patroller.

I. Signs

Temporary condition signs

These signs warn of unusual temporary conditions such as road work zones, diversions, detours, lane closures or traffic control people on the road. They are usually diamond-shaped with an orange background and black letters or symbols.

Here are some common temporary condition signs:

Survey crew working on the road ahead.

Temporary detour from normal traffic route.

Traffic control person ahead. Drive slowly and watch for instructions.

Flashing lights on the arrows show the direction to follow.

Construction work one kilometre ahead.

You are entering a construction zone. Drive with extra caution and be prepared for a lower speed limit.

Road work ahead.

Pavement has been milled or grooved. Your vehicle's stopping ability may be affected so obey the speed limit and drive with extra caution. Motorcyclists may experience reduced traction on these surfaces.

 Lane ahead is closed for roadwork. Obey the speed limit and merge with traffic in the open lane.

 Closed lane. Adjust speed to merge with traffic in lane indicated by arrow.

 Do not pass the pilot or pace vehicle bearing this sign.

 Reduce speed and be prepared to stop.

Portable changeable message sign: Reduce speed as indicated and prepare for changing conditions as described by the sign.

I. Signs

Information and direction signs

These signs tell you about distances and destinations. They are usually rectangular with a green background and white letters. Other signs with different colours guide you to facilities, services and attractions.

Here are some common information and direction signs:

Shows directions to nearby towns and cities.

Shows the distances in kilometres to towns and cities on the road.

Various exit signs are used on freeways. In urban areas, many exit ramps have more than one lane. Overhead and ground-mounted signs help drivers choose the correct lane to exit or stay on the freeway.

Advance signs use arrows to show which lanes lead off the freeway. Signs are also posted at the exit.

Emergency response signs

Some information signs include a numbering system along the bottom of the sign to assist emergency vehicles in determining an appropriate route.

Sometimes one or more lanes may lead off the freeway. The arrows matching the exit lanes are shown on the advance sign in a yellow box with the word 'exit' under them.

Freeway interchanges or exits have numbers that correspond to the distance from the beginning of the freeway. For example, interchange number 203 on Highway 401 is 203 kilometres from Windsor, where the freeway begins. Distances can be calculated by subtracting one interchange number from another.

The term 'VIA' is used to describe the roads that must be followed to reach a destination.

 These signs change according to traffic conditions to give drivers current information on delays and lane closures ahead.

 Shows route to passenger railway station.

 Shows route to airport.

Shows route to ferry service.

 Shows facilities available such as fuel, food, accommodation or camping.

Shows types of fuel available: D — diesel; P — propane; N — natural gas.

 Shows facilities that are accessible by wheelchair.

I. Signs

Other signs

Here are some other common signs:

The slow-moving vehicle sign is orange with a red border. Motor vehicles moving slower than 40 km/h must show this sign at the rear when driving on a road, unless they are only crossing it.

The new driver sign has a green background with black lettering. Placed in the back window of a vehicle, it tells other drivers that the driver is a novice.

Bilingual signs

Watch for these signs when driving in designated bilingual areas. Read the messages in the language you understand best. Bilingual messages may be together on the same sign or separate, with an English sign immediately followed by a French sign.

II. Traffic lights

Traffic lights guide drivers and pedestrians through intersections and along roads. They tell road users when to stop and go, when and how to turn and when to drive with extra caution.

Green light

A green light means you may turn left, go straight or turn right after yielding to vehicles and pedestrians already in the intersection. When turning left or right you must yield the right-of-way to pedestrians crossing the intersection.

Yellow light

A yellow — or amber — light means the red light is about to appear. You must stop if you can do so safely; otherwise, go with caution.

Red light

A red light means you must stop. Bring your vehicle to a complete stop at the stop line if it is marked on the pavement. If there is no stop line, stop at the crosswalk, marked or not. If there is no crosswalk, stop at the edge of the sidewalk. If there is no sidewalk, stop at the edge of the intersection.

Wait until the light changes to green and the intersection is clear before moving through it.

Unless a sign tells you not to, you may turn right on a red light only after coming to a complete stop and waiting until the way is clear. You may also turn left on a red light if you are moving from a one-way road into a one-way road, but you must come to a complete stop first and wait until the way is clear.

Lights and arrows to help turning vehicles

Flashing green lights and green arrows direct drivers who are turning.

Advance green light or arrow

When you face a flashing green light or a left-pointing green arrow and a green light, you may turn left, go straight ahead or turn right from the proper lane. This is called an advanced green light because oncoming traffic still faces a red light.

Pedestrians must not cross on a flashing green light unless a pedestrian signal tells them to.

II. Traffic lights

Simultaneous left turn

When a left-turn green arrow is shown with a red light, you may turn left from the left-turn lane. Vehicles turning left from the opposite direction may also be making left turns because they too face a left-turn green arrow.

After the left-turn green arrow, a yellow arrow may appear. This means the green light is about to appear for traffic in both directions. Do not start your left turn. Stop if you can do so safely; otherwise, complete your turn with caution.

You can still turn left when the light is green, but only when the way is clear of traffic and pedestrians. If the light turns red when you are in the intersection, complete your turn when it is safe.

Pedestrians must not cross on a left-turn green arrow unless a pedestrian signal tells them to.

Transit Priority Signals

Traffic and pedestrians must yield to public transit vehicles at a transit priority signal. The round signal is on top of a regular traffic signal and shows a white vertical bar on a dark background. This allows transit vehicles to go through, turn right or left, while all conflicting traffic faces a red light.

Fully protected left turn

Some intersections have separate traffic lights for left-turning traffic and for traffic going through the intersection or turning right.

When a left-turn green arrow appears for traffic in the left-turn lane, traffic going straight ahead or turning right will usually see a red light. You may turn left from the left-turn lane when you face a green arrow. Vehicles from the opposite direction may also be turning left.

After the left-turn green arrow, a yellow light appears for left-turning vehicles only.

After the yellow light, a red light appears for left-turning vehicles only. Traffic going straight ahead or turning right will face a green light or green arrows pointing straight ahead and to the right.

In these intersections, you may not begin turning left after the green light appears for traffic going straight ahead or turning right. If the light turns yellow while you are in the intersection, complete your turn with caution.

II. Traffic lights

Flashing red light

You must come to a complete stop at a flashing red light. Move through the intersection only when it is safe.

Blank traffic lights

During an electrical power loss, traffic lights at intersections will not work. Yield the right-of-way to vehicles in the intersection and to vehicles entering the intersection from your right. Go cautiously and use the intersection the same way you would use an intersection with all-way stop signs.

Traffic beacons

A traffic beacon is a single flashing light hung over an intersection or placed over signs or on obstacles in the road.

Flashing red beacon

A flashing red beacon above an intersection or stop sign means you must come to a complete stop. Move through the intersection only when it is safe to do so.

Flashing yellow beacon

A flashing yellow beacon above an intersection, above a warning sign or on an obstruction in the road, warns you to drive with caution.

Flashing yellow light

A flashing yellow light means you should drive with caution when approaching and moving through the intersection.

III. Pedestrian signals

Pedestrian signals help pedestrians cross at intersections with traffic lights. The signal for pedestrians to walk is a white walking symbol. A flashing or steady orange hand symbol means pedestrians must not begin to cross.

A pedestrian facing a walk signal may cross the road in the direction of the signal. While crossing, pedestrians have the right-of-way over all vehicles.

Where there are pedestrian pushbuttons, a pedestrian must use the button to bring on the walk signal. Pedestrian signals give people more time to cross than regular traffic lights.

A pedestrian facing a flashing or steady hand symbol should not begin to cross the road. Pedestrians who have already begun to cross when the hand signal appears, should go as quickly as possible to a safe area. While they are crossing, pedestrians still have the right-of-way over vehicles.

At intersections with traffic lights where there are no pedestrian signals, pedestrians facing a green light may cross. Pedestrians may not cross on a flashing green light or a left-turn green arrow.

Intersection pedestrian signals

On a busy main road, an intersection pedestrian signal helps people to cross the road safely by signalling traffic to stop. The intersection pedestrian signal has one or more crosswalks, pedestrian walk and don't walk signals, push buttons for pedestrians, and traffic signal lights on the main road only. Stop signs control traffic on the smaller, less busy crossroad.

You must observe, obey the traffic rules, and use safe driving skills to drive through these intersections. See the section on driving through intersections on page 32.

IV. Pavement markings

Pavement markings work with road signs and traffic lights to give you important information about the direction of traffic and where you may and may not travel. Pavement markings divide traffic lanes, show turning lanes, mark pedestrian crossings, indicate obstacles, and tell you when it is not safe to pass.

Diagram 3-1

Yellow lines separate traffic travelling in opposite directions. White lines separate traffic travelling in the same direction.

Diagram 3-2

A solid line at the left of your lane means it is unsafe to pass. ('A' should not pass.)

Diagram 3-3

A broken line at the left of your lane means you may pass if the way is clear. ('A' may pass if there are enough broken lines ahead to complete the pass safely.)

(Diagram 3-4: Above) Broken lines that are wider and closer together than regular broken lines are called continuity lines. When you see continuity lines on your left side, it generally means the lane you are in is ending or exiting and that you must change lanes if you want to continue in your current direction. Continuity lines on your right mean your lane will continue unaffected.

IV. Pavement markings

Diagram 3-5

Diagram 3-6

Diagram 3-7

A stop line is a single white line painted across the road at an intersection. It shows where you must stop. If there is no stop line marked on the road, stop at the crosswalk, marked or not. If there is no crosswalk, stop at the edge of the sidewalk. If there is no sidewalk, stop at the edge of the intersection.

A crosswalk is marked by two parallel white lines painted across the road. However, crosswalks at intersections are not always marked. If there is no stop line, stop at the crosswalk, marked or not. If there is no crosswalk, stop at the edge of the sidewalk. If there is no sidewalk, stop at the edge of the intersection.

A white arrow painted on a lane means you may move only in the direction of the arrow.

Diagram 3-8

Diagram 3-9

A pedestrian crossing — or cross-over — is marked by two white double parallel lines across the road with an X in each lane approaching it. Stop before the line and yield to pedestrians.

Two solid lines painted on the pavement guide traffic away from fixed objects such as bridge piers or concrete islands. Yellow and black markings are also painted on the objects themselves as warnings.

KEEPING YOUR DRIVER'S LICENCE

Diagram 4-1

Ontario has a one-piece plastic driver's licence. The licence card has a digitized photograph and signature of the driver and a magnetic information stripe. All drivers in Ontario should have a one-piece licence card.

You must carry your licence with you whenever you drive.

Keeping your driver's licence

Renewing your licence

You will get a renewal application form in the mail. Take the form into any of the Driver and Vehicle Licence Offices in the province. They are all equipped to take photographs. You will be asked to sign the form, show identification, pay a fee and have your photograph taken. You will get a temporary licence on the spot and your permanent one will be mailed to you. Carry it with you whenever you drive.

If you do not get a renewal application form in the mail when your licence is due for renewal, call the Ministry of Transportation. You are responsible for making sure you have a valid driver's licence. You can renew an expired car or motorcycle driver's licence within one year without taking any tests.

If your licence has been suspended, cancelled or expired for more than three years, you will be required to reapply for a licence in Ontario and meet all the requirements of graduated licensing including passing all the required tests.

If you are a senior driver, 80 years or older, you must renew your driver's licence every two years. To do this, you must go to a Driver Examination Centre, you must pass a vision test and a test of your knowledge of the rules of the road and traffic signs. You must also attend a group education session dealing with issues that face older drivers. For example, you will learn how the physical changes of aging can affect your driving and what you can do to reduce your risk of collisions as a result of those changes. You may also be asked to take a road test if there is a chance you may pose a safety risk. There is no charge for the tests and the group education session. You only have to pay the licence renewal fee.

Graduated licensing requalification

Under graduated licensing, novice drivers (Class G1, G2, M1and M2) progress through a two-step licensing process by completing the mandatory time periods for each level and passing the required road tests. Except for Class M1, novice drivers have five years to complete the graduated licensing process. However, if your Class G1, G2 or M2 licence is about to expire and you have not completed the process, you can regain or retain the same class of licence by passing a test and paying the five-year licensing fee. This is called 'requalification.' A notice is sent to Class G1, G2 and M2 drivers before their licence expiry date to inform them of their options. If you do not complete the graduated licensing process or requalify before your G1, G2 or M2 licence expires, you will not have a licence to drive.

Changing your name or address

You must tell the Ministry of Transportation within six days of changing your name or address.

You will need a new licence when you change your address. Take the change of information to a Driver and Vehicle Licence Office or mail it to the Ministry of Transportation, P.O. Box 9200, Kingston, ON, K7L 5K4. The ministry will send you a new licence. When you get it, destroy your old licence and carry the new one with you whenever you drive.

When your name changes, you need a new licence. Take the documents you must show (see the chart on this page) and your current licence to a Driver and Vehicle Licence Office. A new photograph will be taken. You will get a temporary licence to use until your permanent licence is mailed to you. Carry it with you whenever you drive.

There is no charge for getting a new licence because you change your name or address.

The chart on this page shows the documents you will need to change the name on your driver's licence. If you don't have them, the ministry will look at your case individually.

Driver's licence laws

It is illegal to lend your licence or let someone else use it. It is also illegal to have an altered licence, to use another licence as your own, or to have more than one Ontario driver's licence.

REASON FOR NAME CHANGE	DOCUMENTATION REQUIRED
Marriage	Marriage certificate
Common-law alliance	Notarized affidavit of the fact
Adoption	Adoption papers
Under the Change of Name Act	Change of name certificate

The demerit point system

The demerit point system encourages drivers to improve their behaviour and protects people from drivers who abuse the privilege of driving. Drivers convicted of driving-related offenses have demerit points recorded on their records. (See the point system table on page 104.) Demerit points stay on your record for two years from the date of the offence. If you collect enough demerit points, you can lose your driver's licence.

New drivers

As a Level One or Level Two driver, you will have your licence suspended if you collect nine or more demerit points during a two-year period.

You will be sent a warning letter after two or more demerit points. At six points, you may have to go to an interview to discuss your record. If you don't go to the interview, your licence may be suspended. At nine points, your licence will be suspended for 60 days.

After the suspension, the number of points on your record will be reduced to four. Any extra points could again bring you to the interview level. If you reach nine points again, your licence can be suspended for six months.

Probationary drivers

Drivers who got their licences before April 1, 1994 must complete two years of probation before becoming fully licensed. Probationary drivers are automatically suspended if they collect six demerit points. You will be reminded of this by letter the first time you get demerit points. Your licence is suspended for 30 days from the time you hand it over to the Ministry of Transportation. You can lose your licence for up to two years if you fail to hand over your licence.

When the suspension is over, all points are removed from your driver's record and a new probationary period begins. You will stay on probation until you complete two one-year periods without being suspended. If your probationary period lasts more than three years you may be asked to complete a Level Two road test to become a fully licensed driver.

Fully licensed drivers

If you collect six demerit points, you will be told about your record and urged to improve your driving habits.

At nine points, you may have to go to an interview to discuss your record and give reasons why your licence should not be suspended. You may also have to complete a driver re-examination. If you fail this test, your licence can be cancelled. If you fail to attend an interview, or fail to give good reasons for keeping your licence, your licence may be suspended.

At 15 points, your licence will be suspended for 30 days from the date you hand over your licence to the Ministry of Transportation. You can lose your licence for up to two years if you fail to hand over your licence.

After the suspension, the number of points on your driver's record will be reduced to seven. Any extra points could again bring you to the interview level. If you reach 15 points again, your licence will be suspended for six months.

TABLE OF OFFENCES

Here are the demerit point penalties for driving offences.

7 points

- Failing to remain at the scene of a collision
- Failing to stop for police

6 points

- Careless driving
- Racing
- Exceeding the speed limit by 50 km/h or more
- Failing to stop for a school bus

5 points

- Driver of bus failing to stop at unprotected railway crossing

4 points

- Exceeding the speed limit by 30 to 49 km/h
- Following too closely

3 points

- Exceeding the speed limit by 16 to 29 km/h
- Driving through, around or under a railway crossing barrier
- Failing to yield the right-of-way
- Failing to obey a stop sign, traffic light or railway crossing signal
- Failing to obey the directions of a police officer
- Driving the wrong way on a divided road
- Failing to report a collision to a police officer
- Improper driving where road is divided into lanes
- Crowding the driver's seat
- Going the wrong way on a one-way road
- Driving or operating a vehicle on a closed road
- Crossing a divided road where no proper crossing is provided

2 points

- Failing to lower headlight beam
- Improper opening of a vehicle door
- Prohibited turns
- Towing people — on toboggans, bicycles, skis, for example
- Failing to obey signs
- Failing to stop at a pedestrian crossing
- Failing to share the road
- Improper right turn
- Improper left turn
- Failing to signal
- Unnecessary slow driving
- Reversing on a divided high-speed road
- Driver failing to wear a seat belt
- Driver failing to ensure that a passenger less than 23 kg is buckled into seat belt or child safety seat
- Driver failing to ensure passenger under 16 years wearing seat belt

Other ways to lose your licence

You may also lose your licence for the following reasons:

Medical suspension

By law, all doctors must report the names and addresses of everyone 16 years or older who has a condition that may affect their ability to drive safely. Addiction to alcohol or drugs are conditions that affect your ability to drive. Doctors report this information to the Ministry of Transportation and it is not given to anyone else. Your driver's licence may be suspended until new medical evidence shows that the condition does not pose a safety risk.

Discretionary HTA suspensions

Your licence **may** be suspended:
- If you don't tell the truth:
  - in an application, declaration, affidavit or paper required by the Highway Traffic Act, its Regulations or the Ministry of Transportation.
  - about vehicle liability insurance.
- If you fail to insure your vehicle.
- If you are convicted of some driving offenses, included careless driving and driving 50 km/h or more over the speed limit.

Mandatory HTA suspensions

Your licence **will** be suspended:
- If you are convicted of failing to stop for a police officer and the court believes you wilfully avoided police during pursuit — that you tried to escape the police. (Your licence will be suspended for five years.)
- If you don't pay a traffic fine when ordered by the court.

Administrative suspension

Your licence will be suspended **immediately** for 90 days:
- If you fail or refuse to give a breath or blood sample when asked by police.
- If your blood alcohol concentration is more than 80 milligrams in 100 millilitres of blood (.08).

This suspension takes effect while you are still at the roadside or at the police station. It is an administrative suspension by the Registrar of Motor Vehicles and is separate from any criminal charges or prosecution which may also take place.

Other ways to lose your licence

Novice driver violations

Drivers holding G1, G2, M1 or M2 licences must follow the specific rules for their class of licence. If you violate any of the graduated licensing conditions for your class of licence, your licence will be suspended for 30 days. This suspension takes effect from the time you surrender your licence on or after the date of the suspension. You can lose your licence for up to two years if you fail to hand over your licence.

Your licence will be cancelled:

- If you fail a driver's re-examination.
- If you don't pay your reinstatement fee.
- If your cheque for licence fees is not honoured by your bank.
- If you voluntarily surrender your driver's licence to the Ministry of Transportation or it is surrendered or returned by another jurisdiction.

Criminal Code suspensions

You will receive a one-year licence suspension the first time you are convicted of a Criminal Code offence. If you are convicted of a second Criminal Code offence, your licence will be suspended for three years. A third Criminal Code offence will get you a lifetime suspension from driving with the possibility of reinstatement after 10 years. Fourth time offenders convicted of a Criminal Code offence are suspended from driving for life with no possibility of reinstatement. Convictions will remain on your driver's record for a minimum of 10 years. The court can order a longer suspension if it believes that keeping you off the road will improve safety.

Your licence will be suspended if you are convicted of any of the following Criminal Code offences:

- Driving or having care and control of a vehicle while your ability is impaired by alcohol or drugs
- Refusing to submit to a breath test for alcohol
- Failing or refusing to provide a breath sample for roadside testing
- Driving or having care and control of a vehicle when your blood alcohol concentration is more than 80 milligrams per 100 millilitres of blood (.08)
- Failing to remain at the scene of a collision to escape criminal or civil liability
- Dangerous driving
- Causing bodily harm by criminal negligence
- Causing death by criminal negligence.

Remedial Measures

If you are convicted of a driving-related Criminal Code offence, you must complete a remedial program before you can get your licence back. There are two types of remedial programs:

- If you are convicted of a drinking and driving related Criminal Code offence, you must take the impaired driving program called Back on Track, delivered by the Centre of Addiction and Mental Health. The three-part program, which is available across the province, involves assessment, education or treatment and follow-up. You must pay the cost of the program directly to the program provider.
- If you are convicted of a non-drinking and driving related Criminal Code offence and have no previous alcohol related convictions, you must undergo a Ministry of Transportation driver improvement interview.

If you have not completed your remedial program by the time your Criminal Code suspension expires, your licence will be further suspended until you have completed the remedial requirements.

Reinstatement fees

Suspended drivers must pay $100 to have their licence reinstated. This fee does not apply to reinstatement following a medical or administrative suspension of your driver's licence.

Driving under suspension

You may not drive, under any circumstances, when your licence is suspended. If you are convicted of driving while your licence is suspended for an HTA offence, you will have to pay a fine of $1,000 to $5,000 for a first offence and $2,000 to $5,000 for a 'subsequent' offence. (A 'subsequent' offence is when you are convicted again within five years.) You may

have to spend six months in jail, or you may have to pay a fine or do both. Your licence will be suspended for an additional six months.

There is a fine for driving when your licence is cancelled.

If you are found guilty of driving while your licence is suspended for a Criminal Code offence, you face a fine of $5,000 to $25,000 for a first offence and $10,000 to $50,000 for a subsequent offence within five years. You also face an additional suspension (one year for a first offence; two years for a subsequent offence) under the HTA and up to two years in prison and three years licence suspension under the Criminal Code.

Driving while prohibited

This is a prohibition order under the Criminal Code conviction. When convicted of violation of order, you will get a suspension of one year for

Other ways to lose your licence

a first offence or two years for a subsequent offence. Courts can order longer prohibition, which will be matched in length by a suspension under the Highway Traffic Act.

Vehicle Impoundment Program

If you are caught driving while your licence is suspended for a Criminal Code offence, the vehicle you are driving will be impounded. This applies whether the vehicle is borrowed from a friend or family member, used for business or employment purposes, rented or leased. The vehicle will be placed in an impound yard for a minimum of 45 days. The owner of the vehicle must pay the towing and storage costs before the vehicle will be released. This program applies to all motor vehicles including passenger vehicles, motorcycles, trucks and buses.

The Vehicle Impoundment Program makes vehicle owners responsible for ensuring that anyone driving their vehicles is not suspended for a Criminal Code conviction. People loaning or renting their vehicles can verify that a driver's licence is valid by phone at 1-900-565-6555 or online at www.mto.gov.on.ca/english/dandv/catalogue.htm. You can also get a driver's abstract at Driver and Vehicle Licence Offices or Service Ontario Kiosks. There is a nominal fee for each licence checked.

Impaired driving

Impaired driving, which means driving when your ability is affected by alcohol or drugs, is a crime in Canada. If you are impaired, you can be convicted of several offences under the Criminal Code of Canada. Your vehicle does not even have to be moving; you can be charged if you are impaired behind the wheel, even if you have not started to drive.

Alcohol

Drinking and driving is a deadly combination.

All drivers, especially inexperienced drivers, must be able to concentrate on driving. That's why the graduated licensing system does not allow new drivers to drink any alcohol when they are going to drive.

Even one drink can reduce your ability to concentrate, to watch out for and react to things that happen suddenly when you are driving. With more alcohol in your blood, you could have trouble judging distances and your vision may become blurred. Factors like fatigue, your mood, and how long ago you ate and how much, can make a difference in how alcohol affects your driving ability.

The police have the right to stop any driver they suspect is impaired. They may also do roadside spot checks. When you are stopped by the police, you may be told to blow into a machine that tests your breath for alcohol — a roadside screening device. If you refuse, you will be charged under the Criminal Code. The police will also notify the Registrar of Motor Vehicles and your licence will be suspended immediately for 90 days.

If the reading on the machine shows you have been drinking, you may be taken to a police station for a breathalyser test. The breathalyser uses your breath to measure the amount of alcohol in your bloodstream.

If you cannot give a breath sample for some reason, the police officer can ask you to let a doctor take a blood sample instead. If you are injured and cannot give your consent, a justice of the peace may authorize a doctor to take a blood sample.

The maximum legal blood alcohol concentration for fully licensed drivers is 80 milligrams in 100 millilitres of blood (.08). Any more than .08 is against the law.

If your reading is less than .08 but .05 or more, or if you register 'warn' on a roadside screening device, the police can suspend your licence for 12 hours. This keeps you from driving until your blood alcohol level drops. You must give your licence to the police officer on demand. The police will tell you when the 12-hour suspension will end and where to get your licence back. Meanwhile, if there is no one else available to drive and no safe place to park your vehicle, it will be towed at your expense.

If your blood alcohol concentration is more than 80 milligrams in 100 millilitres of blood (.08), you will be charged under the Criminal Code. The police will also notify the Registrar of Motor Vehicles and your licence will be suspended immediately for 90 days. Even if your blood alcohol concentration is less than .08, you can still be charged with impaired driving under the Criminal Code.

Level One and Level Two drivers must have a blood alcohol level of zero when driving. New drivers caught drinking and driving will get a 30-day suspension for violating a condition of their Level One or Level Two licence. They can also be charged under the Criminal Code.

Other ways to lose your licence

Drugs

Any drug that changes your mood or the way you see and feel about the world around you will affect the way you drive. The Criminal Code and HTA suspensions apply to drivers impaired by alcohol or drugs.

Illegal drugs such as marijuana and cocaine are not the only problem. Some drugs that your doctor may prescribe for you and some over-the-counter drugs can also impair your driving. Here are some points you should remember:

- If you use prescription medicines or get allergy shots, ask your doctor about side effects such as dizziness, blurred vision, nausea or drowsiness that could affect your driving.
- Read the information on the package of any over-the-counter medicine you take. Any stimulant, diet pill, tranquillizer or sedative may affect your driving. Even allergy and cold remedies may have ingredients that could affect your driving.
- Drugs and alcohol together can have dangerous effects, even several days after you have taken the drug. Do not take a chance — ask your doctor or pharmacist.

Consider the consequences

Having your licence suspended is not the only cost of impaired driving. Depending on whether it is your first, second, third or fourth offence, you can be fined, sent to jail for up to five years and prohibited from driving for the rest of your life.

For impaired driving that causes injury or death, the penalties are even more severe. If you are convicted of impaired driving causing bodily harm, you may be sentenced to up to 10 years in prison. Impaired driving causing death can carry a sentence of up to 14 years in prison.

If you have been drinking and driving and are involved in a collision, your insurance company may not have to pay for damage to your vehicle. If you are injured in the collision, your medical and rehabilitation costs may not be covered.

If you drive for a living, a licence suspension could mean losing your job. And when you do get your licence back, you may find your insurance costs 50 to 100 per cent more for at least three years.

YOUR VEHICLE

All motor vehicles on Ontario roads must be registered, insured and maintained to meet certain basic safety standards. If you own a vehicle, you are responsible for making sure it meets the requirements. People who buy and sell vehicles also have certain responsibilities.

I. Maintaining your vehicle

It is illegal to drive a vehicle in dangerous condition. But maintaining your vehicle also makes sense from an economic point of view: it can mean better mileage and a better price when you sell your vehicle. Maintaining your vehicle also helps to protect the environment.

A police officer or Ministry of Transportation inspector can examine your vehicle, its equipment and any trailer attached to it, at any time. If the vehicle is found to be unsafe, it may be taken off the road until the problem is fixed. If you refuse to allow the examination, you can be fined up to $1,000. If the vehicle is then found to be unsafe, your licence plates can be taken away.

The following types of regular maintenance will help keep your vehicle fit and safe.

Diagram 5-1

Daily or weekly checks

- Keep your vehicle clean, inside and out. Keep seat belts clean to prevent dirt and moisture from damaging the mechanism.
- Check tire pressure. Properly inflated tires mean better mileage and safer driving. Also, check tires for damage or wear.
- Check that all lights are working.
- Check that windshield wipers are properly attached to wiper blades. If your wiper blades leave streaks on the window, replace them.
- Check under the hood when the engine is cold. Check that there is enough oil, water in the radiator, windshield washer fluid, brake fluid and battery fluid, if appropriate. Check all hoses for cracks or leaks and check fan belts for wear or slackness.

Regular service

- Change oil and filter
- Change transmission fluid

- Change axle differential oil
- Check drive and axle shafts
- Check steering, brake and clutch reservoirs
- Check cooling system levels
- Check brake system
- Check front suspension, including alignment and condition of ball joints, steering rods, shock absorbers and springs
- Check engine adjustments — valve clearances, ignition timing, distributor and spark plugs
- Check carburettor or fuel injection system and air filter element
- Check headlight aim.

Winter maintenance

A well-maintained vehicle will generally start in all weather conditions. However, whenever possible, shelter your vehicle from direct contact with rain or snow when it is parked because even the best maintained vehicle can't run if the engine is soaked.

Carry emergency supplies. These should include a shovel, a bag of sand or kitty litter, booster cables, emergency flares or warning lights, blanket and chain for towing. Always carry extra windshield washer fluid in the winter and refill the container when necessary.

Cold weather puts extra strain on your vehicle's systems. With lights, heater, defroster and radio all working at once, batteries do not get a good charge at idle speed. If idling in traffic for long periods, shift to neutral and rev the engine gently. Have your battery checked and terminals cleaned at least twice during the winter.

Faulty exhaust systems are especially dangerous in the winter when drivers are more likely to drive with windows and vents closed. Have your exhaust checked if it sounds noisy or rattles.

I. Maintaining your vehicle

Tires

The type of tires you have and the way they are made are critical for good traction, mileage and safety. Keep these points in mind when you buy or replace tires, and check your vehicle owner's manual or the tire manufacturer's guide for recommendations.

Tires must meet standards described in the Motor Vehicle Tire Safety Act.

- Replace tires when the tread is less than 1.5 millimetres deep or when tread wear indicators touch the road. Vehicles that weigh more than 4,500 kilograms must replace their front tires when tread is less than three millimetres deep.
- Replace tires with bumps, bulges, knots, exposed cords, or tread and sidewall cuts deep enough to expose cords (Diagram 5-2).
- Any tire on a vehicle must not be smaller than the vehicle manufacturer's specified minimum size. And it must not be so large that it touches the vehicle or affects its safe operation.
- Use similar tires on all four wheels. Some combinations are illegal, including: radial-ply tires on the front and bias-ply or belted bias-ply on the rear; a mix of 50 or 60 series tires on the front with any other mixture on the rear; and a combination of types or sizes on the same axle, unless the types and sizes are equivalent by industry standards. This does not apply to a single spare tire used in an emergency.
- The pressure of the spare tire should be the same as the pressure of the tire with the highest pressure.
- Any tire with the wording "not for highway use," "farm use only," "competition circuit only," "NHS," "TG," "SL" or any other words that mean the tire is not for use on the road must not be used on a vehicle that travels on roads.

- Although snow tires or all-weather tires are not required by law, they give the best traction for vehicles in winter. Install snow tires at least on the drive wheels. Four snow or all-weather tires are best for vehicles in snowbelt areas.

Diagram 5-2

- Studded tires are illegal in Ontario.
- Scrap tires are a serious environmental concern. Proper tire maintenance will extend the life of a tire and delay its disposal. Some tips for longer wear: maintain the right air pressure; inspect tires for wear; rotate tires regularly; and practise good driving habits.

II. Vehicle insurance and registration

Insurance

Ontario has compulsory automobile insurance. This means every vehicle registered in the province must be insured.

You must show proof that you have insurance coverage before you can register a vehicle or renew your registration. If you do not tell the truth about your insurance or if you show false documents, you can be fined $500 to $2,500. You may also lose your driver's licence for up to one year and have your vehicle taken away for up to three months.

You must insure all your vehicles for third party liability of at least $200,000. This covers you in the event that you injure or kill someone or damage someone's property. Collision insurance to cover damage to your own vehicle is a good idea but not required by law.

When driving your own vehicle or someone else's, you must carry the pink liability insurance card given to you by the insurance company for that particular vehicle. You must show this card when a police officer asks for it. If you do not, you can be fined up to $200.

Registration

Vehicle registration includes licence plates and a vehicle permit.

Licence plates in Ontario work on a plate-to-owner system. This means that vehicle licence plates move with the vehicle owner, not the vehicle. When you sell or change vehicles, you must remove your plates. If you do not intend to use them on another vehicle, you may return your plates to a Driver and Vehicle Licence Office.

Your vehicle permit must have an accurate description of your vehicle. This means that if you change anything about your vehicle, such as the colour, you must report it at a Driver and Vehicle Licence Office within six days.

If you own a vehicle and you change your name or address, you must notify the Ministry of Transportation within six days. You can do this in person at a Driver and Vehicle Licence Office or by mail, using the change of information stub attached to your vehicle permit.

New residents

New Ontario residents have 30 days to register their vehicles. To get a vehicle permit and Ontario licence plates, go to a Driver and Vehicle Licence Office. You must bring along:

- A Safety Standards Certificate.
- Proof of insurance.
- A K-22 customs card if you have brought the vehicle in from another country.
- The vehicle permit, or ownership, from where you used to live.

III. Buying or selling a used vehicle

If you are selling a used vehicle privately in Ontario, you must buy a Used Vehicle Information Package. This applies to the private sale of any car, van, light truck, motor home or motorcycle. The package is available from any Driver and Vehicle Licence Office or through the the Ministry of Consumer and Commercial Relations.

The package, which the seller must show to potential buyers, has a description of the vehicle, its registration and lien history in Ontario, and the average wholesale and retail values for its model and year. It also includes information about retail sales tax.

As well as giving the buyer the Used Vehicle Information Package, sellers must remove their licence plates, sign the vehicle transfer portion of their vehicle permit and give it to the buyer. Sellers must keep the plate portion of the permit.

The buyer must take the package and the vehicle portion of the permit to a Driver and Vehicle Licence Office to register as the new owner within six days of the sale.

Before buyers can put their own plates on their new vehicle, they must have:

- their licence plates validated.
- the vehicle portion of the permit issued for the vehicle.
- their own licence plate number recorded on the plate portion of the vehicle permit.
- a valid Safety Standards Certificate.
- the minimum insurance required under the Compulsory Automobile Insurance Act.

Buying and Selling a Used Vehicle in Ontario

Ontario

Safety Standards Certificate

A Safety Standards Certificate is a document that certifies a vehicle's fitness. You can buy and register a vehicle without a safety certificate, but you cannot put your own plates on the vehicle or drive it without one. Any inspection station in Ontario licensed by the Ministry of Transportation can issue a Safety Standards Certificate, provided your vehicle passes an inspection. Many garages are licensed — look for a sign saying it is a Motor Vehicle Inspection Station.

A Safety Standards Certificate is valid for 36 days after the inspection. However, the certificate is not a guarantee or warranty that the vehicle will stay fit for any period.

ONTARIO'S DRIVE CLEAN PROGRAM

Ontario's Drive Clean program is designed to reduce smog-causing emissions from vehicles. Vehicles are responsible for a substantial amount of the pollutants in and around our urban areas, but Drive Clean testing of vehicle emissions can help make a difference in the quality of air we breathe.

If you own a light-duty vehicle that is between three and 20 years older than its model year, you must take your vehicle for a Drive Clean test every two years in order to renew its registration. If you are buying a used vehicle that is older than the current model year, the vehicle must be tested to transfer the ownership and put licence plates on it.

You don't have to wait for a Drive Clean test, to do something positive for the environment. Keeping your vehicle well maintained according to the manufacturer's recommended service schedules is an important part of driving clean. For example, if the 'check engine' or 'service engine' lights come on, have your engine looked at by a qualified service technician as soon as possible. Otherwise, you could face costly repairs to the vehicle's engine or emissions control system.

For more information on Ontario's Drive Clean program, visit www.driveclean.com or call the Drive Clean Call Centre toll-free at 1-888-758-2999.

IV. Towing

Towing a trailer

For more detailed information on towing trailers, including driving techniques and the special licensing and lighting requirements, refer to Towing a Trailer Behind a Car, Van or Small Truck in the Off-Road Vehicles section in this handbook.

Towing disabled vehicles

If your vehicle breaks down, you should get help from a tow truck designed to tow vehicles. If you must use another vehicle to tow, use warning signals or emergency flashers and make sure you attach the vehicles securely. Someone must sit in the disabled vehicle and use the brakes to keep the tow cable tight. If the engine cannot run, don't tow vehicles that have power braking and steering. Without the engine, braking and steering is difficult and towing may lead to a collision.

Trying to start a disabled vehicle by towing is dangerous and could damage both vehicles.

Refer to the Off-Road Vehicles section in this Handbook.

THE LEVEL TWO ROAD TEST

6

Statistics show that new drivers of all ages are far more likely than experienced drivers to be involved in serious or fatal collisions.

To help new drivers develop better, safer driving habits, Ontario introduced graduated licensing in 1994 for all drivers applying for their first car or motorcycle licence. Graduated licensing lets you gain driving skills and experience gradually, in lower-risk environments. The two-step licensing system takes at least 20 months to complete and includes two road tests. Passing the Level Two (G2) road test gives you full Class G driving privileges.

While the Level One road test deals with basic driving skills, the Level Two road test deals with advanced knowledge and skills that are generally gained with driving experience. When you take the test, the examiner will give you directions. As you complete the driving tasks, the examiner will watch to make sure you successfully perform the actions associated with them.

The G2 road test includes a component of expressway driving. Prior to the G2 road test, you must complete a "Declaration of Highway Driving Experience" to ensure that you have sufficient expressway driving experience in order to proceed with the road test.

To proceed with the road test, you must "declare" by signing a form, how many times in the three months before the road test that you have driven on a 400 series highway and/or on a highway with a speed limit of at least 80km/hr. You are required to indicate what was the average length of these trips (i.e. under 5 km, between 5 and 15 km, over 15 km). The 400 series highways include: 400, 401, 402, 403, 404, 405, 406, 407, 409, 410, 416, 417, 420, 427, Queen Elizabeth Way (QEW), Don Valley Parkway (DVP), Gardiner Expressway, E. C. Row Expressway and the Conestoga Parkway. If you do not have sufficient driving experience, the road test will be rescheduled at no charge so that you may gain the necessary experience.

To help you prepare, this chapter tells you the various tasks and actions that you will be expected to perform in your Level Two road test. This is only a guide. For more information on the driving tasks, you should review chapters 2 and 3. The book Road Worthy can also help.

I. Left and right turns: The approach

This driving task begins when the examiner tells you to make a left or right turn and ends at the point just before you enter the intersection. Make sure you take the following actions:

Traffic check   Before slowing down, look all around you. Use your mirrors to check traffic behind you.
If you change lanes, remember to check your blind spot by looking over your shoulder.

Lane   Move into the far left or far right lane as soon as the way is clear.

Signal   Turn on your signal before slowing down for the turn unless there are vehicles waiting to enter the road from sideroads or driveways between you and the intersection. Wait until you have passed these entrances so that drivers will not think you are turning before the intersection.

Speed   Steadily reduce speed as you approach the turn. In a vehicle with manual transmission, you may downshift into a lower gear as you slow down. Do not coast with your foot on the clutch pedal.

Space   While slowing down, keep at least a two- to three-second distance behind the vehicle in front of you.

If stopped

You will need to do this driving task if you cannot complete your turn without stopping, either because the way is not clear or you face a stop sign or red traffic light. Remember to follow these actions:

Stop

Come to a complete stop. Do not let your vehicle roll forward or backward. When traffic conditions allow, move forward to check that the way is clear or to start the turn. If you have to stop after you have passed the stop line, do not back up.

Space

When stopped behind another vehicle at an intersection, leave enough space to pull out and pass without having to back up. Leaving this space protects you in three ways: it lets you pull around the vehicle in front if it stalls; it helps prevent you from being pushed into the vehicle ahead if you are hit from behind; and it reduces the risk of collision if the vehicle ahead rolls backward or backs up.

Stop line

If you are the first vehicle approaching an intersection with a red light or stop sign, stop behind the stop line if it is marked on the pavement. If there is no stop line, stop at the crosswalk, marked or not. If there is no crosswalk, stop at the edge of the sidewalk. If there is no sidewalk, stop at the edge of the intersection.

Wheels

When waiting to make a left turn, keep your front wheels straight. With your wheels turned left, your vehicle could be pushed into oncoming traffic. When waiting to turn right, keep the wheels straight if there is a risk of being pushed into pedestrians crossing the intersection. At a large intersection with curved sidewalks where you are turning right, angle your vehicle to follow the curb so that no other vehicle can fit between you and the curb.

I. Left and right turns:

The driving task involves your actions as you make the turn. Remember to do the following:

Traffic check — If you are stopped, waiting for a green light or for the way to be clear, keep checking traffic all around you. Just before entering the intersection, look left, ahead and right to check that the way is clear. If there is any doubt about the right-of-way, try to make eye contact with nearby drivers or pedestrians. If it is possible for another vehicle to overtake you while you are turning, check your blind spot before starting to turn. You have not properly checked traffic if another vehicle or pedestrian has the right-of-way and must take action to avoid your vehicle.

Both hands — Use both hands to turn the steering wheel throughout the turn. You are most at risk from other traffic when turning. Using both hands on the wheel gives you maximum steering control when you need it most. An exception to this is if you have a disability that prevents you from using both hands.

Gears — In a vehicle with manual transmission, do not shift gears during the turn. If you need to, you may shift gears immediately after the vehicle is moving but before it is well into the turn. You may also shift gears in an intersection wider than four lanes if not doing so would slow down other traffic. Generally, not changing gears gives you more control over your vehicle when turning.

Speed — Move ahead within four to five seconds after it is safe to start. Make the turn at a steady speed, increasing speed as you complete the turn. Drive slow enough to keep full control of your vehicle without slowing down other traffic.

Turn into the corresponding lane on the intersecting road without going over any lane markings or curbs.

Completing the turn

This driving task completes the turn. It begins when you enter the intersecting road and ends when you return to normal traffic speed. Take the following actions:

Lane

End your turn in the lane that corresponds to the lane you turned from. If you are turning left onto a multi-lane road, return to normal traffic speed and move into the curb lane when it is safe to do so. If you are turning right onto a road where the right lane is blocked with parked vehicles or cannot be used for other reasons, move directly to the next available lane.

Traffic check

As you return to normal traffic speed, check your mirrors to become aware of the traffic situation on the new road.

Speed

Return to normal traffic speed by accelerating smoothly to blend with the traffic around you. In light traffic, accelerate moderately. In heavier traffic, you may have to accelerate more quickly. In a vehicle with manual transmission, shift gears as you increase speed.

II. Stop intersection: **The approach**

This driving task is done at intersections where you must come to a stop. It begins at the point where you can see the intersection and ends just before you enter the intersection. Be sure to follow these actions:

Traffic check   Before slowing down, look all around you. Use your mirrors to check traffic behind you.

Speed   Steadily reduce speed as you approach the intersection. In a vehicle with manual transmission, you may downshift into a lower gear as you slow down. Do not coast with your foot on the clutch pedal.

Space   While slowing down, keep at least a two- to three-second distance behind the vehicle in front of you.

The stop

This driving task includes the actions you take while stopped and waiting to move through the intersection.
Remember these points:

Stop

Come to a complete stop. Do not let your vehicle roll forward or backward. When traffic conditions allow, move forward to check that the way is clear or start across the intersection. If you have to stop after you have passed the stop line, do not back up.

Space

When stopped behind another vehicle at the intersection, leave enough space to pull out and pass without having to back up. Leaving this space protects you in three ways: it lets you pull around the vehicle in front if it stalls; it helps prevent you from being pushed into the vehicle ahead if you are hit from behind; and it reduces the risk of collision if the vehicle ahead rolls backward or backs up.

Stop line

If you are the first vehicle approaching an intersection with a red light or stop sign, stop behind the stop line if it is marked on the pavement. If there is no stop line, stop at the crosswalk, marked or not. If there is no crosswalk, stop at the edge of the sidewalk. If there is no sidewalk, stop at the edge of the intersection.

II. Stop intersection: Driving through

This task includes the actions you take as you drive through the intersection and return to normal traffic speed. Make sure to follow these actions:

Traffic check If you are stopped, waiting for a green light or the way to be clear, keep checking traffic all around you. Just before entering the intersection, look left, ahead and right to check that the way is clear. If there is any doubt about the right-of-way, try to make eye contact with nearby drivers or pedestrians. You have not properly checked traffic if another vehicle or pedestrian has the right-of-way and must take action to avoid your vehicle.

Both hands Keep both hands on the steering wheel as you drive through the intersection. You are most at risk from other traffic when you are crossing the intersection. Using both hands on the wheel gives you maximum steering control when you need it most. An exception to this is if you have a disability that prevents you from using both hands.

Gears In a vehicle with manual transmission, do not shift gears crossing the intersection. If you need to, you may shift gears immediately after the vehicle is moving but before it is well into the intersection. You may also shift gears in an intersection wider than four lanes if not doing so would slow down other traffic. Generally, not changing gears gives you more control over your vehicle.

Traffic check As you return to normal traffic speed, check your mirrors to become aware of the traffic situation after you have gone through the intersection.

Speed

Move ahead within four to five seconds after it is safe to start. Return to normal traffic speed by accelerating smoothly to blend with the traffic around you. In light traffic, accelerate moderately. In heavier traffic, you may have to accelerate more quickly. In a vehicle with manual transmission, shift gears as you increase speed.

III. Through intersection: **The approach**

This driving task is done at intersections where you may not need to stop. It begins at the point where you can see the intersection and ends just before the entrance to the intersection. Remember to do the following:

Traffic check   As you approach the intersection, look left and right for traffic on the intersecting road.
If you have to slow down for the intersection, check your mirrors for traffic behind you.

Speed   Keep at the same speed as you go through the intersection unless there is a chance traffic may cross the intersection in front of you. If so, slow down or hold your foot over the brake, ready to slow down or stop. Watch for pedestrians about to cross the intersection and vehicles edging into the intersection or approaching at higher speeds.

Space   Keep at least a two- to three-second distance behind the vehicle in front of you.

Driving through

This driving task includes your actions from the time you enter the intersection until you have crossed it and are returning to normal traffic speed. Remember these points:

Lane

Do not go over lane markings or change lanes in the intersection. If your lane is blocked by a vehicle turning left or a vehicle edging into the intersection from the right, slow down or stop instead of pulling out to go around the vehicle.

Both hands

Keep both hands on the steering wheel as you drive through the intersection. You are most at risk from other traffic when you are crossing the intersection. Using both hands on the wheel gives you maximum steering control when you need it most. An exception to this is if you have a disability that prevents you from using both hands.

Gears

In a vehicle with manual transmission, do not shift gears crossing the intersection. If you need to, you may shift gears immediately after the vehicle is moving but before it is well into the intersection. You may also shift gears in an intersection wider than four lanes if not doing so would slow down other traffic. Generally, not changing gears gives you more control over your vehicle.

Traffic check

If you slowed down for the intersection, check your mirrors again before returning to normal traffic speed.

IV. Freeway: Entering

This driving task begins on the entrance ramp to a freeway and ends when you have reached the speed of the traffic on the freeway. Remember to do the following:

Traffic check

While on the ramp, as soon as you can see freeway traffic approaching from behind, check your mirrors and blind spot for a space to merge safely. At the same time, watch any vehicles in front of you on the ramp and keep back a safe distance. Continue to divide your attention between watching in front, checking your mirrors and looking over your shoulder to check your blind spot until you can merge safely with traffic.

Signal

If you have not done so already, turn on your signal as soon as traffic on the freeway is able to see your vehicle on the ramp.

Space

While on the ramp and merging with freeway traffic, keep at least a two- to three-second distance behind the vehicle in front of you. Time your merge so you do not move in beside another vehicle or into the blind spot of another vehicle. If traffic is heavy or moving at such a high speed that it is difficult to keep an ideal following distance, adjust your speed to get the best spacing possible. While on the ramp and in the acceleration lane, keep inside the lane markings.

Speed

On the curve of the entrance ramp, keep your speed slow enough so that objects and people inside your vehicle are not pushed from the force created by turning the curve. While in the acceleration lane, increase your speed to match that of freeway traffic. While merging, control your speed to blend smoothly with freeway traffic.

Merge　　　　Merge with freeway traffic in a smooth, gradual movement to the centre of the nearest freeway lane.

Cancel signal　　Turn off your signal as soon as you have merged with freeway traffic.

IV. Freeway: Driving along

This driving task checks your actions driving along the freeway but not merging, changing lanes or exiting. Be sure to remember the following points:

Traffic check
While driving along, keep checking traffic all around you and look in your mirrors every five to 10 seconds.

Speed
Avoid exceeding the speed limit or driving unreasonably slowly. Whenever possible, drive at a steady speed. Look ahead to where you are going to be in the next 12 to 15 seconds for dangerous situations or obstacles that you can avoid by changing your speed.

Space
Always keep at least a two- to three-second distance behind the vehicle in front of you. If another vehicle follows too closely behind you, give yourself even more room in front or change lanes. Try to keep a space on both sides of your vehicle and try not to drive in the blind spots of other vehicles. Avoid driving behind large vehicles. Because of their size, they block your view of traffic more than other vehicles.

Exiting

This driving task begins when you are driving in the far right lane of the freeway and can see the exit you want to take. It ends when you reach the end of the exit ramp. Remember to do the following:

Traffic check Before moving into the exit lane, look left and right and check your mirrors. If there is a lane of traffic on your right, such as an acceleration lane from an entrance ramp, or a paved shoulder, remember also to check your right blind spot.

Signal Turn on your signal before you reach the exit lane.

Exit lane Enter the exit lane at the beginning of the lane with a smooth, gradual movement. Stay inside the lane markings. If there are two or more exit lanes, do not cross solid lines on the pavement to change lanes.

Speed Do not slow down before you are completely in the exit lane. Once you are in the lane, slow gradually without causing traffic to pile up behind you. On the curve of the exit ramp, keep your speed slow enough so that objects and people inside your vehicle are not pushed from the force created by turning the curve. In a vehicle with manual transmission, downshift as you reduce speed.

Space Keep at least a two-to three-second distance behind the vehicle in front of you.

Cancel signal Turn off your signal once you are on the exit ramp.

V. Lane change:

This driving task begins as you look for a space to change lanes and ends when you have completed the lane change. Remember to follow these actions:

Traffic check

While waiting to change lanes safely, look all around you. Divide your attention between watching in front, watching the mirrors, and checking your blind spot. If there is another lane beside the one you are moving into, check traffic in that lane to avoid colliding with a vehicle moving into the lane at the same time as you do.

Signal

Turn on your signal when there is enough space for you to change lanes. After signalling, check your blind spot one more time before starting to move into the other lane. Your signal should be on soon enough to give traffic behind you time to react to the signal. If traffic in the lane you are moving into is heavy, you may turn on your signal before there is enough space to change lanes. This will let traffic behind you know that you are looking for a space to change lanes.

Space

Keep at least a two- to three-second distance behind the vehicle in front of you. If there is another lane beside the one you are moving into, be careful not to move in beside another vehicle or into the blind spot of another vehicle.

Speed

Adjust your speed to match the speed of traffic in the new lane.

Change   Change lanes with a smooth, gradual movement into the centre of the new lane.

Both hands   Keep both hands on the steering wheel as you change lanes. Using both hands on the wheel gives you maximum steering control. An exception to this is if you have a disability that prevents you from using both hands.

Cancel signal   Turn off your signal as soon as you have changed lanes.

VI. Roadside stop: The approach

This driving task begins when the examiner tells you to stop and ends once you have come to a stop. Make sure you take these actions:

Traffic check

Before slowing down, check your mirrors for traffic behind you. If there is a chance of traffic or pedestrians overtaking you on the right, check your right blind spot just before pulling over.

Signal

Turn on your signal before slowing down unless there are vehicles waiting to enter the road from sideroads or driveways between you and the point where you intend to stop. Wait until you have passed these entrances so that drivers will not think you are turning before the stopping point.

Speed

Steadily reduce speed as you approach the stop. In a vehicle with manual transmission, you may downshift into a lower gear as you slow down. Do not coast with your foot on the clutch pedal.

Position

Stop parallel to the curb and not more than about 30 centimetres away from it. If there is no curb, stop as far as possible off the travelled part of the road. Do not stop where you will block an entrance or other traffic.

The stop

This driving task includes the actions you take after stopping. Remember to do the following:

Signal   Turn off your signal and turn on your four-way flashers.

Park   If your vehicle has an automatic transmission, put the gear selector in park and set the parking brake. If your vehicle has a manual transmission, set the parking brake and shift into neutral if not turning off the engine, or shift into low or reverse if turning off the engine. When parking on a hill, turn your wheels in the appropriate direction to keep your vehicle from rolling.

VI. Roadside stop: Resume

This driving task begins when the examiner tells you to move back onto the road and ends when you have returned to normal traffic speed. Take the following actions:

Start   Turn on the engine. Release the parking brake and select the correct gear to move back onto the road.

Signal   Turn off your four-way flashers and turn on your left turn signal.

Traffic check   Just before pulling away from the stop, check your mirrors and your left blind spot.

Speed   Return to normal traffic speed by accelerating smoothly to blend with the traffic around you. In light traffic, accelerate moderately. In heavier traffic, you may have to accelerate more quickly. In a vehicle with manual transmission, shift gears as you increase speed.

Cancel signal   Turn off your signal as soon as you are back on the road.

VII. Curve

This driving task begins when the curve comes into sight and ends when you have gone completely around it. Follow these actions:

Speed

As you approach the curve, try to determine the safe speed for the curve. To do this, look for clues such as a sign that shows the safe speed, the shape of the curve and the type of road you are driving on. Slow down to the safe speed for the curve by the time you are 30 metres into it. In a blind curve where you cannot see all the way around it, drive more slowly in case oncoming traffic wanders into your lane or the curve is tighter than you expected. **Slow down before the start of the curve to avoid braking in the curve.** While in the curve, keep your speed steady and slow enough so that objects and people inside your vehicle are not pushed from the force created by turning on the curve. Near the end of the curve, begin accelerating to return to normal speed. In a vehicle with manual transmission, do not shift gears in the curve. Not changing gears gives you more control over your vehicle and reduces the risk of your wheels locking while downshifting.

Lane

As you enter the curve, look as far around it as possible. This helps you stay in a smooth line and centred in the lane throughout the curve. If you look only at the road directly in front of you, you are likely to wander back and forth across the lane, forcing you to constantly correct your steering.

VIII. Business section

This driving task is done on straight sections of road where a number of businesses are located. Be sure to do the following actions:

Traffic check

In a business area, there are many places other than intersections where vehicles or pedestrians are likely to enter the road. These include entrances to businesses, institutions and construction sites, as well as pedestrian and railway crossings. At all these locations, look left and right to check for vehicles or pedestrians about to enter the road.

Mirror check

While driving along, check your mirrors every five to 10 seconds. Check your mirrors more often in heavy traffic or where vehicles are moving at different speeds.

Lane

Drive in the safest lane for through traffic. This is usually the curb lane. However, if the curb lane is blocked by traffic or there are many curbside hazards, the centre lane may be a safer choice. Keep to the centre of the lane and within the lane markings. Look ahead to where you will be in the next 12 to 15 seconds for dangerous situations or obstacles that you can avoid by changing lanes.

Speed

Avoid exceeding the speed limit or driving unreasonably slowly. Whenever possible, drive at a steady speed. Look ahead to where you will be in the next 12 to 15 seconds for dangerous situations or obstacles that you can avoid by changing your speed.

Space

Keep at least a two- to three-second distance behind the vehicle in front of you. Increase the distance if another vehicle follows too closely behind you. On a multi-lane road, try to keep a space on both sides of your vehicle and try not to drive in the blind spots of other vehicles. In slow traffic, avoid driving behind large vehicles that block your view of traffic ahead of you. When you stop behind another vehicle, leave enough space to see its rear wheels or to pull around it without having to back up.

IX. Residential section

This driving task is done on straight sections of residential or rural road.
Remember these points:

Traffic check

On a residential road, watch out for entrances to schools, pedestrian crossings, driveways, sidewalks and any other locations where there might be traffic hazards. On a rural road, watch for entrances to residences, farms, businesses and industrial sites. At all these locations, look left and right to check for vehicles or pedestrians about to enter the road.

Mirror check

While driving along, check your mirrors every five to 10 seconds. Check your mirrors more often in heavy traffic or where vehicles are moving at different speeds.

Lane

Keep to the centre of the lane. If there are no lane markings, keep to the centre of the travelled part of the road, away from parked vehicles or pedestrians. Where you cannot see far ahead on the road because of a curve or a hill, move right to avoid colliding with an oncoming vehicle that is over the centre line. Look ahead to where you will be in the next 12 to 15 seconds for dangerous situations or obstacles that you can avoid by changing lanes.

Speed

Avoid exceeding the speed limit or driving unreasonably slowly. Whenever possible, drive at a steady speed. Look ahead to where you will be in the next 12 to 15 seconds for dangerous situations or obstacles that you can avoid by changing your speed.

Space

Keep at least a two- to three-second distance behind the vehicle in front of you. Increase the distance if another vehicle follows too closely behind you. In slow traffic, avoid driving behind large vehicles that block your view of traffic ahead. When you stop behind another vehicle, leave enough space to see its rear wheels or to pull around it without having to back up.

X. Parallel park: **The approach**

This driving task begins when the examiner tells you to park and ends when you have come to a stop, ready to back into the parking space. Remember these points:

Traffic check   Before slowing down, check your mirror for traffic behind you. Before pulling into position to back up, check your blind spot.

Signal   Turn on your signal before slowing down unless there are vehicles waiting to enter the road from sideroads or driveways between you and your stopping point. Wait until you have passed these entrances so that drivers will not think you are turning before your parallel parking position.

Speed   Steadily reduce speed. In a vehicle with manual transmission, you may downshift into a lower gear as you slow down. Do not coast with your foot on the clutch pedal.

Stop   Stop beside — or parallel to — the parked vehicle (real or imaginary) in front of the empty parking space. Leave at least 60 centimetres between your vehicle and the parked vehicle. Stop when your vehicle is completely in front of the empty parking space.

Park

This driving task includes the actions you take to park in a parallel parking space. Remember to do the following:

Traffic check

Before backing up, look all around the vehicle and check your mirrors and both blind spots. Do not start reversing until the way is clear or traffic has stopped to let you park.

Back up

Begin reversing into the space, turning the steering wheel towards the curb. When your vehicle is about halfway into the space, steer to bring your vehicle in line with the curb. Once you are in the parking space, move forward or backward to fit within the pavement markings or to allow room for the vehicle in front or behind you to pull out. Do not hit the curb or touch another vehicle while entering your parking space. Where there is no curb, park off the travelled part of the road.

Park

If your vehicle has an automatic transmission, put the gear selector in park and set the parking brake. If your vehicle has a manual transmission, set the parking brake and shift into neutral if not turning off the engine, or shift into low or reverse if turning off the engine. When parking on a hill, turn your wheels in the appropriate direction to keep your vehicle from rolling.

X. Parallel park: Resume

This driving task begins when the examiner tells you to move from the parking space and ends when you have returned to normal traffic speed. Remember these points:

Start	Turn on the engine. Release the parking brake and select the correct gear to move back onto the road.
Signal	Turn on your signal.
Traffic check	Just before pulling out of the parking spot, check your mirrors and your blind spot.
Speed	Return to normal traffic speed by accelerating smoothly to blend with the traffic around you. In light traffic, accelerate moderately. In heavier traffic, you may have to accelerate more quickly. In a vehicle with manual transmission, shift gears as you increase speed.
Cancel signal	Turn off your signal after you leave the parking space.

XI. Three-point turn: **The approach**

This driving task begins when the examiner tells you to stop and turn your vehicle around. It ends when you have almost stopped, ready to start the turn. Be sure to do the following:

Traffic check

Before slowing down, check traffic in front and behind you. If necessary, check your blind spot before pulling over to the right side of the road to stop.

Signal

Turn on your signal before slowing down unless there are vehicles waiting to enter the road from sideroads or driveways between you and your stopping point. Wait until you have passed these entrances so that drivers will not think you are turning.

Speed

Steadily reduce speed. In a vehicle with manual transmission, you may downshift into a lower gear as you slow down. Do not coast with your foot on the clutch pedal.

Position

Stop so you are parallel to the curb and not more than 30 centimetres away. Where there is no curb, stop as far as possible off the travelled part of the road. Do not stop where you will block an entrance or other traffic.

XI. Three-point turn: Turn around

This driving task includes the actions you take to turn around and ends when you are ready to drive away in the opposite direction. Remember these points:

Traffic check Check your mirrors and your blind spot just before starting the turn. Wait until the way is clear or traffic has stopped to let you turn. Each time you stop while turning, check traffic in both directions.

Signal Turn on your left signal before starting to turn.

Turn around With the steering wheel turned sharply left, move slowly and smoothly across the road. When you have reached the far left side of the road, stop and put your vehicle in reverse. With the steering wheel turned sharply right, reverse so the vehicle is facing in the new direction. Stop and shift into forward gear to move ahead. Use the whole road to make your turn, reversing only once. Do not reverse over the edge or shoulder of the road or into the curb.

Resume

This driving task begins when you are turned around, ready to move ahead and ends when you have returned to normal traffic speed. Make sure you take these actions:

Traffic check   Check your mirrors before increasing speed.

Speed   Return to normal traffic speed by accelerating smoothly to blend with the traffic around you. In light traffic, accelerate moderately. In heavier traffic, you may have to accelerate more quickly. In a vehicle with manual transmission, shift gears as you increase speed.

Road Worthy

Road Worthy is a comprehensive guide to safe driving for new and experienced drivers.

It includes the rules of the road; skills for driving on any road, driving at night and in bad weather; basic vehicle maintenance; jump starting a vehicle; and changing a flat tire.

The text is clear and easy to understand, with many helpful diagrams and photographs.

Road Worthy is used in high school driver education classes in Ontario and by many commercial driving schools.

This book with 168 pages of information will help you maintain your safe driving skills and enhance your driving enjoyment long after you pass your final road test. (Available for purchase by calling Publications Ontario at (416) 326-5300 or 1-800-668-9938. Or visit us at our website at publications.gov.on.ca)

Diagram 5-4

PART TWO:
OFF-ROAD VEHICLES

Introduction

Off-road vehicles, snowmobiles and mopeds are popular forms of recreation for many people in Ontario. They are also necessary for transportation in remote areas and in emergencies. But these vehicles are not toys. If you intend to use them, you must know how they work, how to drive them safely in different situations and how Ontario laws apply to them.

It is important to remember that off-road vehicles are intended for off-road use. Dirt bikes and all-terrain vehicles cannot be driven on public roads, although snowmobiles can be in some areas.

Mopeds and trailers are intended for public roads. However, if you drive a moped, remember that because your vehicle is small, it will be hard for other drivers to see you. You must drive with extra caution. When towing a trailer, make sure your vehicle is in good condition and is the right size and power for the trailer. Follow the rules for trailering and make sure the trailer is properly attached.

Alcohol presents a major risk to your safety and the safety of others whether you are driving a car, motorcycle, snowmobile, off-road vehicle, moped or towing a trailer. Drinking affects your ability to control your vehicle and increases your chances of having a collision.

This section of the handbook contains information about Ontario's laws and safe driving tips for snowmobiles, off-road vehicles, mopeds and trailers. As you read, remember it is a guide only. For official descriptions of the laws, look in the Highway Traffic Act of Ontario and its Regulations, the Motorized Snow Vehicles Act, the Off-Road Vehicles Act, the Trespass to Property Act and the Occupiers' Liability Act of Ontario.

CONTENTS — Part two

DRIVING A SNOWMOBILE

This chapter tells you what you need to know to drive a motorized snow vehicle in Ontario. This includes age and licence requirements, registration, where you can and cannot drive, safety tips, traffic signs and signals and the Snowmobiler's Code of Ethics.

I. Getting ready to drive a snowmobile

What you need to drive a snowmobile in Ontario

You can drive a snowmobile if you have a valid Ontario driver's licence (any class). If you do not have a driver's licence and you are 12 years of age or older, a valid motorized snow vehicle operator's licence will allow you to drive on trails established and maintained by a recreational organization for the use of snowmobiles. However, you must be 16 years of age or older and have a driver's licence or a motorized snow vehicle operator's licence (not both) to drive a snowmobile along or across a public road where snowmobiles are allowed.

A motorized snow vehicle operator's licence is issued by the Ontario Federation of Snowmobile Clubs in co-operation with the Ministry of Transportation. You must successfully pass a snowmobile driver training course to get a licence. (For more information on how to get a motorized snow vehicle operator's licence, see the section Take A Snowmobile Driver Training Course on page 169.)

If you are a visitor to Ontario and wish to drive a snowmobile while you are here, you must have a valid licence that allows you to drive a snowmobile in your home province, state or country.

You must carry your driver's licence or snow vehicle operator's licence when you are driving your snowmobile anywhere other than on your own property. You must show it when asked by a police or conservation officer and give your correct name and address.

If your driver's licence or snow vehicle operator's licence has been suspended, you may not drive any type of vehicle on or off any roads or in any public place.

Registering and insuring your snowmobile

Before driving a snowmobile, it must be registered with the Ministry of Transportation through a Driver and Vehicle Licence Office. This applies to both new and used snowmobiles. If you buy a new snowmobile, the dealer must register it with the Ministry of Transportation on your behalf at a Driver and Vehicle Licence Office within six days of the sale. If you buy a used snowmobile, you must take the bill of sale to a Driver and Vehicle Licence Office within six days of the purchase.

You must pay a fee to register your snowmobile. This is a one-time fee to be paid by the owner of the snowmobile. After registering, you will be given a permit and a registration number decal to display on your snowmobile. Attach the decal to each side of your snowmobile's cowling or engine cover. It should be placed so that the start of the registration number is between 10 and 15 centimetres from the rear of the cowling. If the decal cannot be placed on the cowling because of the design of the vehicle, place the decal on each side of the tunnel, near the reflector light.

Unless you are driving your snowmobile only on your own property or in an area in remote northern or northwestern Ontario that is exempt, you must have a validation sticker on your registration decal. There is an annual renewal fee for the sticker. Place the sticker in the upper right corner of the decal.

You must carry your snowmobile permit with you and show it to a police or conservation officer when asked.

You must also have liability insurance to drive your snowmobile off your own property. Carry the insurance card given to you by the insurance company for the snowmobile and show it when a police or conservation officer asks for it. If someone else uses your snowmobile with your consent, you are both responsible for any penalties, damages or injuries that may occur.

There are separate requirements and rules regarding the operation of trail grooming equipment. Make sure you know what is required before operating grooming equipment.

Wear a helmet

You must wear a helmet whenever you drive or ride on a snowmobile or on any kind of toboggan or sled

towed by a snowmobile. The only exception is when you are on your own land. The helmet must meet the standards approved for motorcycle helmets, or motor assisted bicycle helmets, and must be fastened properly under the chin.

Protect your eyes and face

Always wear a face shield or goggles. A face shield can help prevent windburn, frostbite, sunblindness and watering eyes from the wind. A face shield can also protect your eyes from branches and twigs when driving through wooded areas. Select lightly tinted and shatterproof shields or goggles to match conditions. For example, choose clear plastic for dull, cloudy days and deep yellow for late afternoon when flat light can hide depressions in the snow. Avoid dark tinted shields or goggles, which can restrict your vision.

Make sure your snowmobile is in good condition

Before every trip, check your snowmobile to make sure it is in good working order. Your life may depend upon it. Do the following:

- **Check the steering mechanism.** Turn the handlebars back and forth to make sure the turning is smooth and unrestricted.
- **Check the condition and tension of the motor drive belt.** Change it if necessary or if you are in doubt about its reliability.
- **Check the emergency switch, headlights and tail lights.**
- **Check the battery solution level.**
- **Check the throttle and brake levers.** Make sure they move freely.
- **Check the spark plugs and the tank's fuel level.** Do not use matches or lighter when doing this and never add fuel when the motor is running.

When towing a toboggan, sled or any other kind of vehicle behind a snowmobile, be sure to use a rigid tow-bar and safety chain. For safety, towed vehicles must have reflective material on the front sides, rear sides and rear to make them more visible. Towing is generally not allowed on public roads except to cross the road at a 90-degree angle. This does not apply to a snowmobile being used to free a stuck vehicle, for any emergency rescue or for trail maintenance.

When towing, use rigid tow-bar and safety chain.

Before you drive anywhere, read the owner's manual carefully and keep it in your snowmobile at all times.

Be well prepared for every trip

Carefully preparing for every trip is an important part of safe snowmobiling. Check local weather forecasts and make sure you tell someone where you will be travelling and when you expect to be back. Use the buddy system; do not drive your snowmobile alone.

Take along a first aid kit, a tool kit, an extra ignition key, a drive belt and spark plugs. On long trips, include a compass, trail map, flashlight, hunting knife, hatchet, extra fuel and matches in a waterproof box.

II. Safe and responsible snowmobiling

Where you can and cannot drive

You may drive a snowmobile on your own property, on the private trails of organizations to which you belong, or on private property when you have the owner's permission. You may also drive in public parks and conservation areas, except where prohibited.

You may not drive a snowmobile on certain high-speed roads, including the '400' series of freeways, the Queen Elizabeth Way, the Ottawa Queensway and the Kitchener-Waterloo Expressway. This includes the area around these roads, from fence line to fence line. You may not drive on the serviced section of a road (from shoulder to shoulder) except to cross. When crossing, you must do so at a 90-degree angle.

Except where prohibited, you may drive your snowmobile along public roads, keeping as far away from the road as possible in the section between the shoulder and the fence line. Local municipalities may pass by-laws that regulate or prohibit snowmobiles anywhere within their boundaries, on or off public roads. Make sure you are aware of the by-laws in the municipality where you intend to snowmobile.

You may not drive a snowmobile on railway tracks unless you have permission from the railway track authority.

II. Safe and responsible snowmobiling

Public trails

Ontario's public trails are established and maintained by many snowmobile clubs. They are patrolled by Ontario Provincial Police, municipal police, conservation officers and Snowmobile Trail Officer Patrol (STOP) officers. Some clubs require snowmobiles to have and display a trail permit to drive on their trails. Some other clubs allow their trails to be used without a trail permit. Trails may have signs stating that a trail permit is required. If you are unsure, check with the local snowmobile club to find out if you need a trail permit.

For trails operated by the Ontario Federation of Snowmobile Clubs, you must have and display a trail permit. This includes trails on private property, municipal property and land owned by the government. Some snowmobile trail user groups are exempt from the trail permit requirement. Those who are eligible for exemption and the documents required as proof are included in the trail permits section of the regulations of the Motorized Snow Vehicles Act. Snowmobilers who are exempt must carry the appropriate documents and show them when requested to do so.

For information about trails and trail permits, contact the local snowmobile club or the Ontario Federation of Snowmobile Clubs 12-106 Saunders Road, Barrie, ON L4N 9A8. Phone 705-739-7669; fax 705-739-5005; or e-mail at info@ofsc.on.ca. You can visit the OFSC website at www.ofsc.on.ca

Watch for trail and highway signs.

Do not trespass

You are trespassing if you drive your snowmobile on private property without permission from the owner. You must leave the property immediately after you are told to do so. If you are driving your snowmobile on private property, you must stop and identify yourself when asked by the police, the owner of the property or a representative of the owner.

You may be fined up to $2,000 if you are convicted of trespassing. In addition, you may be ordered to pay damages up to $2,000. Under certain circumstances, you may also be required to pay for the cost of prosecuting. Charges will be laid against the driver of the snowmobile. If the driver is not known, the owner will be charged if the snowmobile was used with the owner's permission.

A copy of the Trespass to Property Act is available through Publications Ontario. Phone (416) 326-5300 or 1-800-668-9938. It is available over the Internet at http://www.gov.on.ca/MBS/english/publications and www.e-laws.gov.on.ca.

It is an offence under the Railway Safety Act to trespass on railway tracks.

Obey the speed limits

You may not drive a snowmobile faster than 20 km/h in any public park or exhibition ground or on any road where the speed limit for other vehicles is 50 km/h or less. You may not drive faster than 50 km/h on snowmobile trails or on any road where the speed limit for other vehicles is more than 50 km/h.

Municipalities may set other speed limits for snowmobiles on public roads, trails and parks within their boundaries. Check municipal by-laws.

Stop for police

You must come to a safe stop when requested by a police officer to do so. If you do not stop, you may have to pay a fine, or go to jail, or both. If you are convicted of failing to stop for a police officer and the court believes you wilfully avoided police during pursuit — that you tried to escape the police — your licence will be suspended for a minimum of five years. You can lose your driver's licence for the rest of your life if anyone is killed or injured as a result of avoiding police.

Report collisions to the police

You must report to the police immediately any collision that results in injury to any person or damage to property apparently exceeding $400.

II. Safe and responsible snowmobiling

Do not drink and drive

Alcohol is a major factor in snow-mobile fatalities.

It is against the law to drive a snowmobile when you are impaired by alcohol or drugs. Under the Canada Criminal Code, if you are driving a snowmobile impaired or if you have a blood alcohol concentration of more than 80 milligrams in 100 millilitres of blood (.08), or if you refuse a breathalyser test, the police will notify the Registrar of Motor Vehicles and your licence will be suspended immediately for 90 days. If you are convicted of a drinking and driving offence you will have a criminal record and may be required to pay a fine. **All your driving privileges will also be suspended.**

You will have a one-year licence suspension the first time you are convicted of a Criminal Code offence. If you are convicted of a second Criminal Code offence, your licence will be suspended for three years. A third Criminal Code offence will get you a lifetime suspension from driving with the possibility of reinstatement after 10 years. Fourth time offenders convicted of a Criminal Code offence are suspended from driving for life with no possibility of reinstatement. Convictions will remain on your driver's record for a minimum of 10 years. The court can order a longer suspension if it believes that keeping you off the road will improve safety.

If your reading is less than .08 but .05 or more, or if you register 'warn' on a roadside screening device, the police can suspend your licence for 12 hours. This keeps you from driving until your blood alcohol level drops. You must give your licence to the police officer on demand. The police officer will tell you when the 12-hour suspension will end and where to get your licence back. Meanwhile, if there is no one else available to drive and no safe place to park your vehicle, it will be towed at your expense.

Practice safe snowmobiling

Driving a snowmobile requires the same attention and alertness that driving any other kind of vehicle does. You must have complete control of your reflexes. If you are a beginner, practice until you can handle the basic driving skills.

Learn how to control your balance on turns by using your weight to control your movements and leaning in the direction you want to turn. Position your body on the snowmobile in a way that will give you the most comfort and control for the conditions in which you are driving. On level ground, sit or kneel with both knees on the seat. On uneven or bumpy ground, stand on the running boards with your knees slightly bent.

On hard-packed snow or ice, reduce your speed because stops and turns are harder to make and you will require greater distance to complete them. When your snowmobile is trapped in deep snow, remember to turn off the motor before you try to get it out of the snow.

Driving on frozen lakes and rivers can be dangerous, sometimes even fatal. If you are in an unfamiliar area, ask local authorities or residents about the ice condition, inlets, outlets, springs, fast-moving current or other hazards. Listen to local radio broadcast warnings by the Ontario Provincial Police about ice conditions. If you must drive over frozen lakes or rivers, you should consider using a buoyant snowmobile suit. It may save your life.

Wherever you are driving, always watch for trail and highway signs and obey them.

III. Snowmobile signals and signs

Hand signals

Signals tell others what you want to do, giving them a chance to slow down, stop or prepare to turn. Use hand signals to signal before stopping, slowing down suddenly or turning. Give the correct signal well before the action and make sure others can see it. These illustrations show nationally recognized hand and arm signals.

Right turn

Raise your left arm to shoulder height with elbow bent.

Left turn

Extend your left arm straight out and point in the direction of the turn.

Stop

Extend your right arm straight up over your head.

Slowing

Extend your left arm out and down the side of your body. Flap your arm up and down to signal caution.

Oncoming snowmobiles

Raise your left arm to shoulder height with your elbow bent and motion left to right over your head, pointing to the right side of the trail.

Snowmobiles following

Raise left arm to shoulder height with your elbow bent. Motion front to back over your shoulder with your thumb, like a hitchhiker.

Last snowmobile in line

With elbow bent, raise your left forearm to shoulder height and clench your fist.

Trail signs

Trail signs give you important information about what to do in certain situations. Here are some common trail signs and what they mean. Because trail signs are not official traffic signs, they may vary in shape and colour. Watch for signs such as these and obey them.

Stop

A stop sign is eight-sided and has a red background with white letters. Come to a complete stop.

Stop ahead

Be prepared to stop for a stop sign up ahead.

Snowmobiling permitted

A sign with a green circle means you may do the activity shown inside the ring. You may drive a snowmobile in the area where this sign is displayed.

Snowmobiling restricted

A sign with a red circle with a line through it means the activity shown inside the ring is not allowed. Do not drive a snowmobile in the area where this sign is displayed.

Direction signs

These signs give you information about the direction in which you should travel on the trail. Do as the sign tells you.

III. Snowmobile signals and signs

Traffic signs

If you are driving your snowmobile along or across any public roads, you need to be aware of traffic signs and what they mean. The following traffic signs relate specifically to snowmobiles.

Snowmobiles permitted
Snowmobiles are allowed on the road or highway where this sign is displayed.

Snowmobiles restricted
Snowmobiles are not allowed on the road or highway where this sign is displayed.

Snowmobiles crossing
This sign warns drivers that snowmobiles are allowed to cross the road.

WIND CHILL FACTOR

It is important to consider wind chill factor when planning winter outdoor activities.

Wind chill factor is the combined effect of wind and low temperature which makes it feel much colder on a windy day in winter than it really is. This is caused by the faster cooling effect of the wind. For example, if the actual temperature is -10°C and the wind speed is 40 km/h the temperature feels like -31°C.

You need to be aware of the wind chill factor so that you can dress appropriately. Also make sure that young passengers are properly dressed and that their hands and face are well protected.

The chart on the next page can help you calculate wind chill so you will be aware of potentially dangerous conditions.

Wind Chill Calculation Chart

Observed wind speed at 10m elevation, in km/h	Air Temperature in °C											
	5	0	-5	-10	-15	-20	-25	-30	-35	-40	-45	-50
5	4	-2	-7	-13	-19	-24	-30	-36	-41	-47	-53	-58
10	3	-3	-9	-15	-21	-27	-33	-39	-45	-51	-57	-63
15	2	-4	-11	-17	-23	-29	-35	-41	-48	-54	-60	-66
20	1	-5	-12	-18	-24	-31	-37	-43	-49	-56	-62	-68
25	1	-6	-12	-19	-25	-32	-38	-45	-51	-57	-64	-70
30	0	-7	-13	-20	-26	-33	-39	-46	-52	-59	-65	-72
35	0	-7	-14	-20	-27	-33	-40	-47	-53	-60	-66	-73
40	-1	-7	-14	-21	-27	-34	-41	-48	-54	-61	-68	-74
45	-1	-8	-15	-21	-28	-35	-42	-48	-55	-62	-69	-75
50	-1	-8	-15	-22	-29	-35	-42	-49	-56	-63	-70	-76
55	-2	-9	-15	-22	-29	-36	-43	-50	-57	-63	-70	-77
60	-2	-9	-16	-23	-30	-37	-43	-50	-57	-64	-71	-78
65	-2	-9	-16	-23	-30	-37	-44	-51	-58	-65	-72	-79
70	-2	-9	-16	-23	-30	-37	-44	-51	-59	-66	-73	-80
75	-3	-10	-17	-24	-31	-38	-45	-52	-59	-66	-73	-80
80	-3	-10	-17	-24	-31	-38	-45	-52	-60	-67	-74	-81

Approximate Thresholds:

Wind chill at or below -25°C:
risk of frostbite in prolonged exposure.

Wind Chill at or below -35°C:
frostbite possible in 10 minutes;
warm skin, suddenly exposed.
(Shorter time if skin is cool at the start.)

Wind Chill at or below -60°C:
frostbite possible in less than 2 minutes;
Warm skin, suddenly exposed.
(Shorter time if skin is cool at the start.)

TAKE A SNOWMOBILE DRIVER TRAINING COURSE

If you are between 12 and 15 years of age, or if you are 16 and older and do not have a valid Ontario driver's licence, you must successfully pass a snowmobile driver training course to get your operator's licence to drive a snowmobile. A snowmobile driver training course can also be a valuable refresher for licensed and experienced snowmobilers.

The course takes about six hours and is usually held over three days. It covers safe driving practices, snowmobile laws, knowledge of the snowmobile, maintenance, driving positions, survival, first aid, night driving, trail signs, clothing and storage. It also teaches safe and courteous driving habits and skills to help you avoid collisions and property damage.

The training course is offered by the Ontario Federation of Snowmobile Clubs (OFSC) in co-operation with the Ministry of Transportation and is offered by club instructors trained by the OFSC. For the location of the nearest OFSC member club offering the course and the cost, contact the OFSC Driver Training Office at 12-106 Saunders Road, Barrie, ON, L4N 9A8. Phone 705-739-7669 or fax 705-739-5005. You can visit the OFSC website at www.ofsc.on.ca.

THE SNOWMOBILER'S CODE OF ETHICS

Follow this code of ethics and you will do your part to make snowmobiling a respectable, fun and safe winter recreation.

1. I will be a good sportsperson and conservationist. I recognize that people judge all snowmobilers by my actions. I will use my influence with other snowmobilers to promote responsible conduct.
2. I will not litter trails or camping areas. I will not pollute lakes or streams. I will carry out what I carried in.
3. I will not damage living trees, shrubs or other natural features.
4. I will respect other people's property and rights.
5. I will lend a helping hand when I see someone in distress.
6. I will make myself and my snowmobile available to assist in search and rescue operations.
7. I will not interfere with or harass hikers, skiers, snowshoers, people who are ice fishing or participating in other winter sports. I will respect their rights to enjoy recreation facilities.
8. I will know and obey all federal, provincial and local rules regulating the operation of snowmobiles in areas where I use my snowmobile.
9. I will not harass wildlife. I will avoid areas posted for the protection of wildlife.
10. I will not snowmobile where snowmobiles are prohibited.

DRIVING AN OFF-ROAD VEHICLE

This chapter tells you what you need to know to drive an off-road or all-terrain vehicle that has not been licensed for use on public roads in Ontario. Off-road vehicles are any two or three-wheeled motorized vehicles, as well as specific vehicles, prescribed by regulations, with four or more wheels intended for recreational use, such as dune buggies.

I. Getting ready to drive an off-road vehicle

What you need to drive an off-road vehicle in Ontario

You must be 12 years of age or older to drive an off-road vehicle except on your own property or under the close supervision of an adult.

While off-road vehicles are generally not allowed on public roads, there are some exceptions. (See the section **Where you can and cannot drive**). If you do drive an off-road vehicle on or across a public road, you must have a valid Ontario driver's licence (any class).

Registering and insuring your off-road vehicle

Off-road vehicles must be registered with the Ministry of Transportation at a Driver and Vehicle Licence Office. This applies to both new and used vehicles. You must be 16 years or older to register an off-road vehicle and you must be able to prove you own the vehicle.

The following vehicles do not need to be registered as off-road vehicles: golf carts, road-building machines, farm vehicles and motorized wheelchairs. In addition, off-road vehicles participating in a rally or exhibition sponsored by a motorcycle association with more than 25 members do not need to be registered for the event.

If you buy a new off-road vehicle, you must get a bill of sale from the dealer.

If you buy a used off-road vehicle, you will need to complete a self-declaration of ownership available from the Driver and Vehicle Licence Office where you go to register. When transferring an off-road vehicle, you should get the vehicle portion of the vehicle permit from the previous owner.

You must pay a fee to register your off-road vehicle. After registering, you will be given a vehicle permit and licence plate. You should carry the vehicle permit at all times unless

you are operating the vehicle on land owned by the owner of the vehicle.

If you have a two- or three-wheeled vehicle, attach the licence plate to the front of the vehicle in plain view. If you have a vehicle with four or more wheels, attach the licence plate to the rear of the vehicle.

You must register your vehicle within six days of becoming the owner. If you change your address, you must notify the Ministry of Transportation in person at a Driver and Vehicle Licence Office or by mail to the Ministry of Transportation, P.O. Box 9200, Kingston, ON, K7L 5K4 withinsix days of the change.

If you are driving your off-road vehicle anywhere other than on your own property, you must also have vehicle liability insurance. You must carry the insurance card with you to show when a police officer asks for it. If someone else uses your off-road vehicle with your consent, you are both responsible for any penalties, damages or injuries that may occur.

Wear a helmet

You must wear a helmet whenever you drive or ride on an off-road vehicle or on any vehicle towed by an off-road vehicle. The only exception is when you are on your own property. The helmet must meet the standards approved for off-road vehicles and should be fastened properly under the chin.

Protect your face and body

Always wear a face shield or goggles. A face shield can help prevent wind-burn, sunblindness and watering eyes from the wind. It can also protect your eyes from branches and twigs when driving through wooded areas. Wear pants that cover your legs and boots that are high enough to cover your ankles. To make yourself more visible to others while driving, wear brightly colored clothing.

Make sure your vehicle is in good condition

Before every trip, check your vehicle to make sure it is in good working order. Your life may depend upon it. Check the vehicle thoroughly before you start to drive, including the following:

- Check the brake control to make sure it moves freely. Adjust if necessary.
- Check that the throttle opens and closes smoothly in all steering positions.
- Check the condition of the tires and tire pressure.
- Check the fuel lines and connections to make sure there are no leaks.
- Check that you have enough fuel.
- Check that the engine is running smoothly. Make sure the vehicle is in neutral before starting the engine.

Before you drive anywhere, read the owner's manual.

Be well prepared for every trip

Carefully preparing for every trip is an important safety measure.

Check local weather forecasts and make sure you tell someone where you will be traveling and when you expect to be back. Use the buddy system; drive with others, not alone. Take along a first aid kit, a vehicle repair kit and an extra ignition key. On long trips, include a compass and maps.

II. Safe and responsible off-road vehicle driving

Where you can and cannot drive

You may not drive an off-road vehicle on public roads. This includes the area between the boundary or property lines, including median, shoulders and ditches.

There are some exceptions. For example, there are some roads that you may drive an off-road vehicle directly across. In addition, vehicles with three or more wheels may be driven along some public roads when they are being used for farming or for licensed hunting or trapping fur-bearing animals. These vehicles must display a slow moving vehicle sign at the rear of the vehicle.

The roads that cannot be driven along are primarily controlled-access freeways, such as the 400 series. For more specific information, you should read the Off-Road Vehicles Act.

Obey the rules

You must stop if a police officer signals you to do so. You can also be stopped by a landowner when you are driving on private property. If signalled to stop by an authorized person, you must stop and, if asked, properly identify yourself.

Everyone who drives an off-road vehicle without care and attention or without reasonable consideration for other people and property may be charged with careless driving. Other offences, such as dangerous driving and alcohol related offences, apply to drivers of off-road vehicles. When you drive an off-road vehicle on a public road, the Highway Traffic Act offences also apply.

Report collisions to the police

You must report to the police immediately any collision that results in injury to any person or damage to property apparently exceeding $1000.

Do not drink and drive

It is against the law to drive an off-road vehicle when you are impaired by alcohol or drugs. Under the Canada Criminal Code, if you are driving impaired or if you have a blood alcohol concentration of more than 80 milligrams in 100 millilitres of blood (.08), or if you refuse a breathalyser test, the police will notify the Registrar of Motor Vehicles and your licence will be suspended immediately for 90 days. If you are convicted of a drinking and driving offence, you will have a criminal record and may be required to pay a fine. Your driver's licence will also be suspended.

Do not carry passengers

Do not carry passengers on an off-road vehicle designed for one person. Carrying passengers changes the weight distribution of the vehicle and limits your ability to shift position on the vehicle for control and stability.

Practice safe driving skills

Driving an off-road vehicle is different than any other vehicle and takes more skill than you might think at first. Be sure to read your owner's manual before you begin to drive.

If you are a beginner, practice driving your vehicle in an open area, free of obstacles, until you become skilled at handling it. Choose ground that is uniform, either dirt, sand or snow. Avoid paved surfaces when driving an off-road vehicle. Off-road vehicles are designed for off-road use and are more difficult to manoeuvre on paved surfaces. When driving, keep both feet on the footrests at all times. Do not try to stabilize a tipping vehicle by putting your foot down. You could run over your foot or leg.

Be extremely careful driving through water. First, check that the water is not too deep. Drive slowly and carefully so you can steer around rocks and other obstacles. Driving fast across unknown water is dangerous. Hidden rocks or holes could throw you off the vehicle and cause serious injury or drowning.

Always use a flag mast when driving in dunes and hills. When driving up hills, remember that you need a running start to climb most hills. Be extra cautious when driving among pedestrians, horseback riders, sunbathers or bicyclists.

Read the Snowmobiler's Code of Ethics (page 172) and follow it when driving your off-road vehicle.

DRIVING A MOPED

This chapter tells you what you need to know to drive a moped or motor-assisted bicycle on public roads in Ontario.

3

I. Getting ready to drive a moped

What you need to drive a moped in Ontario

You must be at least 16 years of age and have a valid Ontario driver's licence (any class) to drive a moped on public roads in Ontario. If you do not have a valid driver's licence, you must pass a vision test and a test of your knowledge of the rules of the road to get a licence to drive a moped.

Registering and insuring your moped

Under the Highway Traffic Act, a moped is a motor-assisted bicycle with the following characteristics:

- Weighs 55 kilograms or less
- Piston displacement is no more than 50 cubic centimetres
- Pedals can be used to propel the moped at all times
- Maximum speed on level ground is 50 km/h within a distance of 2 km from a standing start.

Licence plates are required for mopeds. When registering your moped at a Driver and Vehicle Licence Office, you must show the bill of sale. Dealers of mopeds are required by law to provide purchasers with a certificate that guarantees the moped fits the definition under the Highway Traffic Act.

After registering, you will be given a vehicle permit and licence plate similar to a motorcycle plate. Attach it to the rear of your moped.

You must also have liability insurance for your moped. Carry the insurance card with you to show if a police officer asks for it.

Wear a helmet

You must wear a helmet whenever you drive your moped. The helmet must meet the standards approved for motorcycle helmets and should be fastened properly under the chin. To make yourself more visible to others while driving, wear brightly coloured clothing.

Make sure your moped is in good condition

Before every trip, check your moped to make sure it is in good working order. Before you drive anywhere, read the owner's manual. Use lights, reflectors and reflective tape on your moped to make you more visible to other drivers at night and whenever visibility is poor.

II. Safe and responsible moped driving

Where you cannot drive

You may not drive a moped on high-speed roads such as the 400 series highways, the Queen Elizabeth Way, the Queensway in Ottawa and the Kitchener-Waterloo Expressway. In addition, local municipalities can ban mopeds from roads in their jurisdiction where the speed limit is 80 km or greater.

Do not drink and drive

It is against the law to drive a moped when you are impaired by alcohol or drugs. Under the Canada Criminal Code, if you are driving impaired or if you have a blood alcohol concentration of more than 80 milligrams in 100 millilitres of blood (.08), or if you refuse a breathalyser test, the police will notify the Registrar of Motor Vehicles and your licence will be suspended immediately for 90 days. If you are convicted of a drinking and driving offence, you will have a criminal record and may be required to pay a fine. **All your driving privileges will be suspended.**

You will have a one-year licence suspension the first time you are convicted of a Criminal Code offence. If you are convicted of a second Criminal Code offence, your licence will be suspended for three years. A third Criminal Code offence will get you a lifetime suspension from driving with the possibility of reinstatement after 10 years. Fourth time offenders convicted of a Criminal Code offence are suspended from driving for life with no possibility of reinstatement. Convictions will remain on your driver's record for a minimum of 10 years. The court can order a longer suspension if it believes that keeping you off the road will improve safety.

If your reading is less than .08 but .05 or more, or if you register 'warn' on a roadside screening device, the police can suspend your licence for 12 hours. This keeps you from driving until your blood alcohol level drops. You must give your licence to the police officer on demand. The police officer will tell you when the 12-hour suspension will end and where to get your licence back. Meanwhile, if there is no one else available to drive and no safe place to park your vehicle, it will be towed at your expense.

Do not carry passengers

It is illegal to carry a passenger on a moped.

Practice safe driving skills

Because a moped is small, it can be hard for other drivers on the road to see you. Drive defensively and do everything you can to make yourself visible to others.

Making a turn at a busy intersection can be particularly hazardous on a moped where it is difficult for other drivers to see you. Follow these tips for making safe turns:

- Plan ahead. Do not decide to turn at the last minute.
- Check traffic, signal and move into the proper lane for making the turn.
- Signal your turn well ahead of the turning point and hold the signal until you are ready to start the turn.
- Put both hands on the handlebars when making the turn.
- Complete your turn in the proper lane.

When driving on public roads, you must obey all the rules of the road.

TOWING A TRAILER BEHIND A CAR, VAN OR SMALL TRUCK

This chapter tells you what you need to know to tow a trailer in Ontario. This includes licence and registration requirements, trailer size and characteristics, as well as safety tips to follow when towing a trailer.

Before you attempt to tow a trailer, consider the size, power and condition of your vehicle. Make sure it is capable of towing both the trailer and the load you intend to carry and that your trailer and hitch meet all the requirements described in this chapter.

I. What you need to tow a trailer in Ontario

Licence and permit

You must have a valid driver's licence (Class G1, G2 or G) or higher class of licence to tow a trailer with a gross vehicle weight of up to 4,600 kilograms. If your trailer and load exceeds the size and weight specified in the Highway Traffic Act, you may need a higher class of licence or an oversize vehicle permit to tow it. Oversize permits are available at some Ministry of Transportation Driver and Vehicle Licence Issuing Offices.

It is against the law to tow more than one trailer behind your vehicle.

Registering your trailer

A trailer is considered a separate vehicle. Before you can tow one on any public road, you must register it and pay a one-time registration fee at a Driver and Vehicle Licence Office. When you register your trailer you will receive a licence plate and vehicle permit. Attach the licence plate to the back of your trailer where it is clearly visible. Always carry your permit, or a copy of it, to show to a police officer when asked for it.

Make sure your trailer is in good condition

Your trailer must be in safe operating condition. If it is not, a police officer may remove your trailer from the road until it is made safe to operate.

Brakes

If your trailer has a gross trailer weight, vehicle and load of 1,360 kg or more, it must have brakes strong enough to stop and hold the trailer.

Lights

Your trailer must have:
- a white licence plate light;
- a red tail light; and
- two red reflectors at the rear of the trailer, as far apart as possible.

If your trailer is wider than 2.05 metres, it must also have:

- two yellow clearance lights, one on each side at the front of the trailer, as far apart as possible, to let drivers coming toward you know the width of your trailer; and

- two red clearance lights, or reflectors, one on each side at the rear of the trailer, as far apart as possible, to let drivers behind you know the width of your trailer.

Your trailer must have mudguards, fenders, and flaps or be designed in such a way that it does not spray or splash traffic travelling behind you.

If the load in your trailer blocks your vision to the rear, you must have additional mirrors that provide a clear view of the road to the rear. Load your trailer carefully so that nothing comes loose or falls off while you are moving.

Attaching your trailer

Your trailer must have two separate ways of attaching to your vehicle so that if one fails or comes loose, the trailer will stay attached.

No passengers

You may not carry any person in any trailer, including a house or boat trailer, when it is being towed.

Trailer hitch

Use a good quality trailer hitch. The class of trailer hitch you use depends upon the gross trailer weight — the total weight of trailer and load — of your trailer. Make sure you use the right trailer hitch for the weight of your trailer. It should be securely attached to your vehicle, following manufacturer's recommendations.

The hitch-ball should be installed so that when the trailer is attached and tightened, it is level with no tilting. If the hitch pulls down the rear of your vehicle, you may need to use a load-equalizing trailer hitch. You may also be able to shift some of the load in the trailer to the rear to reduce the load on the rear of your vehicle.

In addition to a ball and hitch, be sure to use safety chains or cables, strong enough to hold the trailer and load, in case the ball and hitch accidentally come apart.

II Safe and responsible trailer towing

Loading your trailer

When loading your trailer, strap everything down, inside, as well as outside, the trailer. It is an offence to have a load that may become dislodged or may fall off. Do not overload your trailer. Too much weight in the trailer can put a strain on your vehicle and damage your tires, wheel bearings and axle. When carrying a boat on a trailer, do not carry cargo in the boat unless your trailer is designed and equipped for the extra weight.

The distribution of the weight in your trailer is also very important. Generally, more of the trailer load should be in front of the trailer axle than behind it for proper hitch weight. About five to 10 per cent of the trailer's total weight should be supported on the hitch, within the weight limit marked on the hitch. Poor load balance can cause your trailer to sway or fishtail. The ball and hitch may also become separated, especially if there is too much weight in the rear of the trailer.

Heavy and improperly placed loads can pull down the rear of your vehicle, lifting the front end and affecting your steering, especially in wet and slippery conditions. It may also affect the aim of your headlights so that your low beams blind approaching drivers. The alignment of your mirrors may also be affected.

Starting out

Before each trip, check the trailer hitch, wheels, tires, lights, load distribution and load security to make sure they are safe. Check your tire pressure with the trailer loaded while the tires are still cold.

When you start to drive, accelerate carefully. Drive slowly and carefully.

Curves and turns

Stay close to the middle of your lane when taking a curve.

When making a right turn, check traffic. Look in your right mirror. Signal and slow down. If the turn is sharp, move ahead until your vehicle's front wheels are well ahead of the curb before turning to the right.

When making a left turn, check traffic. Signal. Proceed slowly. When you make your turn, swing wide by driving well into the intersection before turning.

Slowing down and stopping

A sudden stop can cause your trailer to jackknife or slide sideways or the load to shift. To avoid sudden stops, increase the following distance between you and the vehicle ahead. Keep out of the fast lanes and maintain a speed that will allow you to slowdown and stop smoothly in any situation.

Passing

You cannot accelerate as quickly when you are towing a trailer. You also need more space because the length of your vehicle is much longer with a trailer attached. Before you pass, make sure you have enough time and room to complete the pass. Once you have passed, allow more room before you move back to your lane. Do not cut back into the lane too soon. This can cause your trailer to sway and make it difficult to control.

Being passed

If you are holding up a line of traffic, signal, pull over and let the other vehicles pass. Fast-moving trucks and buses create a strong air disturbance behind them. If a large bus or truck passes you, the wall of wind behind it may whip your trailer to the side, pushing it out of control. When you experience this, do not brake. Carefully steer your vehicle and trailer back into position. A slight increase in speed may help.

Backing up

Back up very slowly and have someone outside the vehicle to direct you. Use a series of small turns to steer. It is a good idea to practice this skill off the road in an empty parking lot until you are comfortable with your ability.

To back up to the right, steer to the left. The front end of the trailer will go left, but the rear end will go right. To back up to the left, steer to the right. The front end of the trailer will go right, but the rear end will go left.

INDEX — PART TWO: OFF-ROAD VEHICLES

Other Official Handbooks for You

Copies of this handbook and others may be purchased from a retail store near you, from a Driver Examination Centre, from a Driver and Vehicle Licence Office or from:

Publications Ontario
50 Grosvenor Street
Toronto, Ontario
M7A 1N8

or by calling
(416) 326-5300
or 1-800-668-9938 (toll free)
(416) 326-5317 (fax)

Prepayment required by cheque or credit card — VISA or Mastercard

THE OFFICIAL DRIVER'S HANDBOOK
INCLUDES OFF-ROAD VEHICLES & TRAILERS
The Official Driver's Handbook $ 12.95
ISBN 0-7794-2718-1

THE OFFICIAL MOTORCYCLE HANDBOOK
INCLUDES OFF-ROAD VEHICLES & TRAILERS
The Official Motorcycle Handbook $ 14.95
ISBN 0-7794-2719-X

THE OFFICIAL TRUCK HANDBOOK
INCLUDES RULES OF THE ROAD & SIGNAGE
The Official Truck Handbook $ 16.95
ISBN 0-7794-2721-1

THE OFFICIAL BUS HANDBOOK
INCLUDES RULES OF THE ROAD & SIGNAGE
The Official Bus Handbook $ 16.95
ISBN 0-7794-2722-X

THE OFFICIAL AIR BRAKE HANDBOOK
NEW, REVISED EDITION
The Official Air Brake Handbook $ 18.95
ISBN 0-7794-2720-3

All prices are subject to 7% G.S.T. and 5% Shipping Costs. Please add 12% to your total purchase to cover G.S.T. and shipping cost.

Personalize your licence plates — with two to eight characters, as well as a great choice of colour graphics. Then you'll really stand out from the crowd.

Turn the page to find out more.

NOW THERE ARE MORE WAYS THAN EVER TO EXPRESS YOURSELF!

WE'RE HELPING YOU BUILD CHARACTERS.

Now you've got extra choices when creating your personalized licence plate. We've introduced seven and eight characters. So you've got even more to work with — a minimum of two characters and right up to eight. Just think of the possibilities.

Every personalized plate is one of a kind. No one else can have the same plate as yours.

For more information and to order your personalized plates, call 1-800-AUTO-PL8 (1-800-288-6758).

**Or visit our website:
www.mto.gov.on.ca:80/english/dandv/vehicle/personlz.htm**
Or drop by your local Driver and Vehicle Licence Office or one of 60 ServiceOntario kiosks.

Gift certificates are available too.

ONTARIO
BCRE8TVE
— YOURS TO DISCOVER —

ONTARIO
NOWYOURS
— YOURS TO DISCOVER —

Graphic licence plates are a hit! And now there are more than 40 choices available. Support your favourite Ontario sports team, community or arts organization, professional group or university. Or select a timeless icon like the loon or trillium.

For a totally unique look, add a colour graphic to a personalized plate with up to six characters.

So express yourself — with colour graphics and personalized licence plates.

For more information and to order your plates, call 1-800-AUTO-PL8 (1-800-288-6758).

Or visit our website: www.mto.gov.on.ca: 80/english/dandv/vehicle/graphic.htm Or drop by your local Driver and Vehicle Licence Office or one of 60 ServiceOntario kiosks.

Gift certificates are available too.

ADD SOME COLOUR WHERE IT COUNTS.

ONTARIO
000SAM
YOURS TO DISCOVER

ONTARIO
000SAM
YOURS TO DISCOVER